Streusel: 2 butter
2 flour
5 sugar

Jim Fobel's Old-Fashioned

BAKING BOOK

OTHER BOOKS BY JIM FOBEL

* BEAUTIFUL FOOD

* THE BIG BOOK OF FABULOUS FUN-FILLED CELEBRATIONS
AND HOLIDAY CRAFTS (with Jim Boleach)

* THE STENCIL BOOK (with Jim Boleach)

Jim Fobel's Old-Fashioned BAKING BOOK

Recipes from an American Childhood

Ballantine Books • New York

Acknowledgment

A very special thank you to my good friend, Brown Cranna,
for his tireless efforts and help in the testing and
retesting of the recipes in this book

Recipes for Aunt Irma's Sour Cream Twists, Aunt Charlotte's Milk Chocolate Cake,
Aunt Myra's Butterscotch Pie, Aunt Marie's Spice Cake, and Grandma Wahlstrom's
Nisua are reprinted by permission from the April, 1982 issue of *Food & Wine
Magazine*. Copyright © 1982 by The International Review of Food & Wine Associates.

Library of Congress Cataloging-in-Publication Data

Fobel, Jim.
Jim Fobel's old-fashioned baking book.

Includes index.
1. Desserts. 2. Baking. I. Title. II. Title:
Old-fashioned baking book.
TX773.F63   1987   641.8'65   87-1230
ISBN 0-345-34822-2

Produced by Jane Ross Associates, Inc. and Bellwether Books.

Designed by Liz Trovato

Manufactured in the United States of America

First Edition: November 1987

10 9 8 7 6 5 4 3 2 1

Dedication

For my grandmother, Hilma Alina, my aunts Myra,
Irma, Charlotte, and Marie, and my mother, Airi, with love

Good cooks are educated people
Schooled at their Aunts' and
Mothers' knees. Instinctively
they behave in kitchens
As in a busy hive behave the bees.
                              Anonymous

❧ Contents ❧

INTRODUCTION

My grandmother, Hilma Alina, baked both a cake and a pie every day of the week, and on Fridays she made bread all day long, enough to last her large family for the entire week. Saturdays were reserved for making her special nisua, a fragrant cardamom-flavored Finnish bread, and on Sundays she entertained a house full of visitors from noon until night. A formidable cook and baker, she presided at every meal at the immense dining-room table in the house on Spruce Street in Ashtabula Harbor, Ohio, where she and my grandfather, George Wahlstrom, had settled. Born in Helsinki, Finland, my grandfather was a musician and conductor who had performed widely in Europe and in this country before meeting my grandmother. After their marriage in 1907, he became director of music for the schools of Ashtabula Harbor, a small Finnish fishing community on the shore of Lake Erie, where the couple raised five daughters—Irma, Marie, Charlotte, Myra, and the youngest, Airi, my mother.

Because my grandfather and all the girls came home from school for lunch, the entire family shared every meal together. Even at lunch, a simpler meal than dinner, the table was laden with my grandmother's homemade pickles, relishes, and preserves, buttered bread and salad, sandwiches and soup or a hot casserole, and a pitcher of farm-fresh milk, followed most often by slices of pound cake and fresh fruit or homemade cookies. My grandfather never failed to get up at the end of every meal to kiss my grandmother and to say to her, "Ali, you outdid yourself; the food was superb."

All the Wahlstrom girls, each wrapped in a different apron (my grandmother prided herself on never making two alike), spent a great deal of time in the kitchen from an early age, learning by instruction and example to cook and bake. But all were banished not only from the kitchen but from the house itself during the critical baking time on the days when grandma made angel food or sponge cake; she prided herself on her cakes being light as clouds, and wasn't about to take the chance that a heavy footfall or banging door would interfere with their airiness.

Summertime was picnic time, and the Wahlstroms organized many Sunday afternoon expeditions to the country. Grandma would make a cake and a pie and roast a couple of chickens or a beef sirloin and bake beans slowly overnight. Marie made the potato salad, Charlotte the cole slaw, and Airi squeezed lemons for the lemonade. Grandma made deviled eggs and stuffed celery while Irma covered the entire dining room table with the makings of a quantity of sandwiches.

Myra was in charge of loading up the Ford touring car with baskets and baskets of food that also included tomatoes, cucumbers, carrots, pickles, olives, corn relish, a big basket of strawberries, and a huge watermelon. Joined by friends who brought along even more food, the Wahlstroms headed a caravan of three or four cars that inevitably had to stop at least once along the country roads for someone to retrieve grandma's big summer hat. The procession would arrive in due course at Farmer Paasenen's; here the assembled group acquired a bucket of ice-cold buttermilk.

The picnic lasted all day. The men tossed horseshoes, the children played in a nearby creek, and the ladies played canasta or bridge or sat in the shade and embroidered. After a tremendous feast and a short rest, they would cover a big table with desserts—grandma's sour cherry pie, Aunt Myra's butterscotch pie, devil's food cake and sponge cake. But the first to disappear was always Mrs. Paasenen's cheese pie, which had a delectable texture somewhere between custard and cheesecake, and was baked within hours after Mrs. Paasenen milked the cow and made the cheese. At the end of the day the caravan wound its way home as the children, exhausted, fell asleep in the backs of the cars.

When my mother married my father, Jack, some years after my grandfather died, she moved with him to the small farming community of Perry, Ohio, a short drive from Ashtabula Harbor. My parents, my brothers, and I lived in a small white two-story house with a peach orchard on Blackmore Road, just down the road from Lake Erie. We kept a flock of chickens in a big coop in the backyard, raising them and selling their eggs. My mother baked her own bread, churned her own butter, and put up her own jams, preserves, and dozens of fruits and vegetables.

Much of my childhood was spent in kitchens—my mother's, my grandmother's, or those of my aunts in Ashtabula. My grandmother always took pity on her small grandsons when they looked wistfully around her kitchen, and she produced wonderful things to eat: Once she whipped up a second cake on the spot after we demolished the first. We and my cousins went from house to house—both Aunt Irma and Aunt Charlotte had settled within a few blocks of grandmother's house on Spruce Street—enjoying the bounty of all the Wahlstrom sisters' passion for baking. On holidays in particular, their tables practically overflowed with food. After a very ample dinner, the children still looked forward eagerly to the desserts: Our particular favorites were Aunt Irma's frosted butter cookies that she made in special shapes for each holiday. There were turkeys at Thanksgiving, hearts on Valentine's Day, pumpkins for Halloween, and for Christmas a wide assortment that included Santa Claus cookies, wreaths with silver balls, and decorated Christmas trees.

After we had finished dinner at Aunt Irma's house it would be time to go on to Aunt Charlotte's, where we would be served cookies and nisua and perhaps one of Aunt Charlotte's special milk chocolate cakes and a banana meringue pie. And of course there were always the traditional apple and pumpkin pies at Christmastime. We children would play on the floor all evening, and the feasting seemed never to end.

Although the happy and carefree days of my childhood are long gone, the memories of good times celebrated with good things to eat are wonderfully vivid still. I have inherited from my mother and from Aunt Irma thousands of recipes, representing my grandmother's, my mother's, and my aunts' zeal in acquiring recipes wherever they went—from friends, family, restaurants, newspapers, magazines, or from a neighbor over the backyard fence. Whenever they tasted something they liked, they asked for the recipe. They recorded these recipes on cards and scraps of paper and in notebooks that date back to 1917. I have some written on penny postcards and others on the backs of beauty parlors' calling cards, all of them now yellow and brown and brittle with age.

When I decided to gather the best of their vast number of baking recipes into a book, I thought the task would be easy: After all, I have spent fifteen years cooking and baking professionally, and these recipes were tried and true. But in fact the process of recreating the desserts as I remember them proved very difficult. After I had read through all of the recipes and selected those I thought best, I embarked on the job of testing them. I wanted to ensure that the ingredients were so precisely indicated and the instructions so clearly written that anyone who followed the recipe faithfully would be able to achieve the desired result. And here is where the difficulty lay.

In the first place, my grandmother and her daughters did not follow recipes to the letter. Invariably, they made alterations—a pinch of this, something else omitted, twice as much of some of the flavorings. Sometimes they noted these changes, but usually they did not. I had learned by watching my mother cook and bake, so I knew that when she measured the teaspoon of vanilla called for in the recipe, she really put in two. I knew that she folded the whipped cream into her lemon chiffon pie because I had seen her do it so many times, yet there is no mention of folding in the original recipe. Filling and frosting recipes were often doubled to make a cake more delicious and extravagant-looking. And occasionally the baking time was changed—Aunt Myra's brownies, for instance, were regularly baked for a shorter time than the recipe specified to make them more moist.

Another of the difficulties facing me was that most of the recipes lacked all or part of the necessary instructions. Since grandmother had taught her daughters in painstaking detail the variety of procedures comprising the art of baking, they found no need to write them down. The techniques were passed on from one to the other and, eventually, to me.

Most of the original recipes called for far too much sugar for today's taste. However, reducing the amount of sugar without sacrificing the flavor and texture of the original recipe proved to be a difficult task, since sugar plays an important role in the structure of baked goods. In order to learn just how much sugar I could safely omit, I generally did a first test for a cake recipe with 25 percent less sugar than called for, then inched this way and that in additional tests until I found the right formula, maintaining the old-fashioned character of the original recipe but eliminating the cloying sweetness.

In carrying out the intensive work on this project, I have been buoyed by the conviction that these carefully collected and cherished family recipes should not remain part of a crumbling file, but should be shared with others. I have taken immense pleasure in recreating these dishes, using as a guide the memory of the way each tasted when lovingly prepared by my mother, my grandmother, or my aunts. It has been greatly rewarding to tease from the yellowed cards and notebook pages and faded handwriting the secrets of grandmother's blackberry cake or Aunt Irma's sour cream twists or mother's peach coffee cake and to savor again the extraordinary desserts I so loved as a child.

INGREDIENTS

FLOUR

ALL-PURPOSE FLOUR. The recipes in this book were tested using Pillsbury's Best XXXX Enriched All-Purpose Flour (bleached), which is generally consistent in quality. The quality of other brands varies considerably from region to region in the United States and these variations can affect the results of the recipes. Gold Medal All-Purpose Flour is also a very reliable choice. Measure flour by first stirring, then lightly spooning it into a dry-ingredient measuring cup and carefully leveling with a knife or spatula. (A dry-ingredient cup measures accurately when filled exactly to its rim; cups for liquid measure have an added lip to allow for the curved upper surface of the fluid.) Do not tap the cup or the flour will settle and the measurement will be off. All-purpose flour does not need to be sifted.

CAKE FLOUR. When cake flour is called for in a recipe, be sure to use 100 percent cake flour only, not self-rising cake flour, which contains other ingredients. The recipes in this book were tested with Swans Down Enriched Bleached Cake Flour. Cake flour is frequently quite compact in the box and therefore must be sifted before measuring. To measure, lightly spoon the sifted flour into a dry-ingredient measuring cup and carefully level off with a knife or spatula, without tapping the cup. Flour may be sifted onto waxed paper or into a bowl. If you cannot find cake flour, you may substitute, for each cup of cake flour, ¾ cup all-purpose flour plus 2 tablespoons cornstarch.

Note: Never use self-rising flour in a recipe unless it is specified. (None of the recipes in this book calls for it.)

SUGAR

GRANULATED SUGAR. Pure cane granulated sugar has been used in all recipes calling for granulated sugar. Measure granulated sugar using dry-ingredient measuring cups, and level with a knife. Superfine sugar, specified in some recipes, has smaller granules and imparts a finer texture to the finished dessert.

CONFECTIONER'S SUGAR. Confectioner's 10-X powdered sugar has been used in recipes calling for confectioner's sugar. Since confectioner's sugar can be very lumpy, always sift it before measuring. To measure, lightly spoon it into a dry-ingredient measuring cup and level it off with a knife.

BROWN SUGAR. Old-fashioned dark brown and light brown pure cane sugars are simply granulated sugar flavored with molasses. Although the recipes in this book specify one or the other type, they are basically interchangeable. But do not substitute the granulated type that will not pack down, or the liquid type. Measure brown sugar by firmly pressing it into a dry-ingredient measuring cup. To keep brown sugar soft, some people add a strip of orange peel to the box and store it, tightly closed, in the refrigerator.

FATS

BUTTER. All recipes in this book call for unsalted or "sweet" butter. Lightly salted butter may be substituted, but the amount of salt in the recipe should be reduced or eliminated. "Softened" butter should not be allowed to become so soft that it is oily. Perhaps a more accurate description of softened butter would be "butter at cool room temperature." A finger pushed into properly softened butter will leave a dent but the butter will remain slightly firm.

VEGETABLE SHORTENING. The recipes in this book were tested using Crisco vegetable shortening. Any similar product should produce the desired results.

LARD. Though I have not used lard in any of the recipes here, occasionally I like to add a little for a true old-fashioned flavor. You may use lard in the flaky pastry if you wish, substituting it measure for measure for the shortening or butter or substituting it for just a couple of tablespoons of the butter or shortening.

YEAST

Recipes calling for yeast were made with active dry yeast. I don't recommend the new fast-acting yeasts because the flavors of the baked product don't develop as well. Fresh yeast can also be used. Substitute one ⅗-ounce cake of fresh yeast for one ¼-ounce package of dry yeast. If you buy active dry yeast in bulk, use one scant tablespoon in place of one ¼-ounce package.

EGGS

USDA grade AA large eggs were used in all of the recipes in this book. Contrary to what you may have heard, it is not necessary to use eggs at room temperature, though in yeast breads cold eggs will slow down the risings. Even here, however, cold eggs may be used, since the dough will rise even in the refrigerator. In whipping egg whites, I have never found any difference between cold whites and those at room temperature. When making meringue, the really important thing is to make sure that the whites contain not a speck of yolk and that the bowl and beaters are impeccably clean and grease-free.

CREAM

Look for a brand of heavy cream, sometimes labeled whipping cream, that is not ultrapasteurized. The "ultra" variety takes a long time to whip and never attains the volume that regular cream does. It also tastes slightly different. In recipes calling for half and half, you may substitute light cream or half cream and half milk.

CHOCOLATE AND COCOA

Baker's All Natural Unsweetened chocolate and Baker's All Natural Semisweet chocolate were used in all recipes calling for chocolate. While Baker's chocolate products are of consistently high quality, you may want to experiment with Ghirardelli's unsweetened chocolate and with fine imported sweetened chocolate like Lindt or Tobler. Wherever cocoa is called for, I used Hershey's cocoa, which is unsweetened. In recipes calling for chocolate chips, use real semi-sweet chocolate such as Nestlé's or Hershey's.

FRUIT

All recipes calling for fresh fruits were tested using farm-fresh produce, in season.

VANILLA

Although all the recipes in this book were tested with commercial vanilla extract, homemade is far superior. The two are interchangeable in most recipes, but since homemade extract can have a stronger flavor, you may want to cut the quantity in half for a more delicate taste in, say, whipped cream.

To make vanilla extract, place one to six vanilla beans (pods) in a tall narrow jar and fill with vodka or half vodka and half commercial vanilla extract. Let steep at room temperature for at least a month and shake before using. Replenish the missing extract with more vodka or commercial extract. Homemade vanilla extract keeps indefinitely.

For special desserts, remove a pod and slit it open lengthwise. Scrape the minuscule seeds into whatever you are making and return the pod to the extract.

NUTMEG

The flavor of freshly grated nutmeg is far superior to ground so I urge you to invest in a small nutmeg grater and a jar of whole nutmegs. Freshly grated nutmeg has been used in all the recipes calling for nutmeg in this book.

POTATO STARCH

Pure potato starch is available in the kosher food section of many supermarkets. Streit's brand is excellent. Potato starch is a wonderful thickener for the bases in old-fashioned buttercreams. It is also used in the Dream Cookies on page 144.

BAKING TIPS

PREPARING PANS AND BAKING SHEETS

When recipes specify greased pans, you have the option of coating them with softened butter or with vegetable shortening. For fine desserts butter should be used, but in most cases vegetable shortening is perfectly satisfactory. There is enough butter in most of the recipes in this book to overwhelm any flavor contribution from vegetable shortening. I frequently use shortening to lightly coat baking sheets or cake pans because it is already soft and I don't have to remember to soften extra butter.

Always start with cool baking sheets for baking. If you want to continue baking immediately after removing the baking sheet from the oven, run cold water over the bottom of the sheet to cool, then dry it and proceed.

CAKE PANS. Along with an array of 8- and 9-inch round cake pans, an 8-inch square pan, a 13-by-9-inch oblong pan, and assorted other sizes, a 10-inch tube pan with removable bottom is very useful. Do *not* buy one with a nonstick surface.

PIE PANS. I have used standard, commonly available, 9-inch metal pie pans for all the pies in this book. There are, however, very shallow ones on the market, also measuring nine inches, and these are inadequate. You need a pan that holds four to four and a half cups, so measure the capacity of yours before you begin. The four-cup pan will be fine for all the recipes in this book.

MEASURING

Dry-ingredient measuring cups come in sets of individual measurement sizes—¼ cup, ⅓ cup, ½ cup, and so on. These enable you to level the top of the measured ingredient with a spatula or a knife. I sometimes use them to measure liquid (very carefully—the liquid can rise higher than the top of the cup, making the measurement inaccurate), but you should never use a liquid cup for measuring dry ingredients.

Liquid-ingredient measuring cups made of glass and plastic have marks printed on the sides, extra space above the top measurement line, and a lip for pouring. Always check the measurement at eye level for accuracy.

Note: Measuring cups can be off by as much as three tablespoons per cup. I was horrified to discover this, because accuracy is critical in baking. Perhaps not surprisingly, many of the new plastic measuring cups are inaccurate, but I have also thrown out many inaccurately printed Pyrex glass cups. To solve this problem, I bought an accurate scientific beaker (school- or medical-supply outlets carry these) and measured every cup in my collection against it. Then I discarded those that were incorrect.

SIFTING

Cake flour and confectioner's sugar pack down in their boxes and must be sifted. Use a conventional sifter or a sieve and measure after sifting by lightly spooning the flour or sugar into a measuring cup and leveling it off with a knife.

FOLDING

To fold together two ingredients such as stiffly beaten egg whites or whipped cream into a custard, first stir a spoonful of the whites or cream into the custard to lighten it, then turn the mixture into the whites or cream. Using a large rubber spatula, cut straight down through the center, turn the spatula toward you and lift up. Turn the bowl slightly and repeat again and again, working as quickly as possible for maximum volume, and continuing only until no streaks of whites or cream are visible.

PROOFING YEAST

Proofing yeast means activating it to determine if it is alive and fresh. Because it is a living organism, yeast responds to changes in its environment, so it is important to control the conditions to which you subject it very carefully. Heat the water to between 105° and 115°F (check the temperature with a thermometer) and stir a little sugar into the water to give the yeast something to feed on as it grows. Sprinkle the yeast over the water's surface and allow it to rest a minute or two, then stir to dissolve the yeast. Set the bowl in a warm, draft-free place. If the yeast does not foam and bubble, doubling in bulk, in about five minutes, or if it reacts sluggishly, discard the yeast and start over. The yeast may have been old, or the water too hot or too cold.

KNEADING

Kneading dough develops the gluten in the flour, and the dough changes from sticky to elastic and satiny as you knead it. This should take about ten minutes on a floured surface. Push, fold, and turn the dough in a systematic pattern as you work. Today many electric mixers come equipped with dough hooks that perform this task with excellent results.

FROSTING CAKES

Always brush loose crumbs from the cake before you begin. If you are plagued with the problem of crumbs getting into the frosting as you work and are using a buttercream frosting (as opposed to a seven-minute or boiled frosting), spread a very thin layer on the cake, just enough to barely coat it, and chill until set. When you are ready to proceed with frosting, the loose crumbs will have adhered to the cake.

To keep the serving plate neat, place four two-inch-wide strips of typing or waxed paper around the rim of the plate and set the cake on top so at least half of each strip protrudes. Carefully pull out the strips after frosting the cake, and the plate will be clean.

TABLE OF EQUIVALENTS

INGREDIENT	MEASURE	WEIGHT
Almonds		
Blanched whole	1 cup	6 oz.
Chopped or slivered	1 cup	5 oz.
Apples, fresh		
1 medium, chopped	1 cup	6 oz.
1 large		6–8 oz.
Apricots, fresh		
8–10 small		1 lb.
Apricots, dried, pitted	1 cup packed	8 oz.
Apricot preserves	1 cup	12-oz. jar
Bananas		
2 medium, mashed	1 cup	
2 large, chopped	2 cups	
Berries, fresh		
1 pint	2 cups	
Butter		
1 stick	8 tablespoons (½ cup)	4 oz.
2 sticks	1 cup	½ lb.
Carrots		
2 medium, peeled and shredded	1 cup	
Cherries, candied	1 cup packed	8 oz.
Cherries, fresh, sour	6 cups	2 lbs.
Chocolate, semisweet or unsweetened		
1 square		1 oz.
Chocolate chips	1 cup	6 oz.
Citrus peel, candied	1 cup packed	8 oz.
Cocoa	1 cup	4 oz.
Coconut, sweetened, shredded	1 cup	about 3 oz.
Dates, pitted and chopped	1 cup	6 oz.
Egg whites		
4 large	½ cup	
8 large	1 cup	

Flour		
All-purpose, sifted	4 cups	1 lb.
Cake, sifted	4½ cups	1 lb.
Hazelnuts, whole	1½ cups	8 oz.
Lemons		
1 medium	3–4 tablespoons juice	
Nectarines, fresh		
2 medium, sliced	1 cup	
Oranges, fresh		
1 medium	6–8 tablespoons juice	
Peaches, fresh		
1 medium		4 oz.
1 large		6–8 oz.
Peanuts, shelled	1 cup	5 oz. (approx.)
Peanut butter	1 cup	9 oz.
Pears, fresh		
1 medium		6 oz.
Pecans, shelled and chopped	1 cup	4 oz.
	¾ cup	3 oz.
	2 tablespoons	½ oz.
Pineapple, candied	1 cup packed	8 oz.
Plums, fresh		
4 medium, sliced	1½ cups	
Poppyseeds	¾ cup whole	4 oz.
Prunes, dried, pitted, chopped	1 cup packed	8 oz.
Pumpkin, fresh	3 cups purée	3 lbs.
Raisins, seedless	1 cup	6 oz.
Rhubarb, fresh, diced	4 cups	1¼ lbs.
Sugar, granulated or superfine	2¼ cups	1 lb.
Sugar, brown	2¼ cups packed	1 lb.
	1 cup packed	7 oz.
Sugar, confectioner's	4½ cups sifted	1 lb.
	3½ cups unsifted	1 lb.
Walnuts, shelled and chopped	1 cup	4 oz.
Yeast, dried	1 scant tablespoon	¼ oz.
Yeast, fresh		
1 cake		⅗ oz.

❧ CAKES ❧

Cakes are to me the most festive of all the wonderful baked desserts to be found in this book. They were made for all important occasions—for birthdays, holidays and anniversaries—as well as for everyday dinners, picnics and all our numerous family gatherings.

Of the countless cake recipes in the family files, I have selected what seem to me the most outstanding. The recipes offered here for marble cake, devil's food cake, silver (white) and gold (yellow) cakes are simply the best there are: I am confident you will never find better ones. And you'll also find many wonderful cakes that I've never seen elsewhere: grandma's blackberry cake, a dense ring cake in which the berries create varicolored stains of red, blue, and purple; oatmeal cake with a unique crunchy topping, one of my all-time favorites; harvest moon cake with its lovely butterscotch flavor; 1933 glory cake with paradise filling, for which dried apricots and fresh bananas are used for the filling and frosting, virtually coating the cake with fruits; carnival cake, its layers flecked with chocolate and its filling a sort of cooked pudding including walnuts.

At the age of twelve I discovered for myself the magic of cake-baking when I decided to make a gold cake as a birthday surprise for my mother. I was so enthralled with the transformation of my newly mixed batter into cake that I stood on a chair to watch the entire proceeding through the window in the oven door. The project almost came to grief when I frosted the cake while it was still too warm and had to run to a neighbor for help as the layers slowly slid apart. Some toothpicks and a short spell in the refrigerator saved the day. To re-create the exact taste of that and the many other splendid cakes I remember so vividly has been a great satisfaction to me, and I hope that you will find them equally memorable.

GRANDMA'S DEVIL'S FOOD CAKE

My grandmother was famous for this light chocolate cake,
its cocoa-rich layers spread with sinfully rich, fudgy frosting. My friends maintain
that it gets even better as it keeps in the refrigerator, but I'll never know for
sure because mine always disappears too quickly to find out.

MAKES ONE 8-INCH 2-LAYER CAKE

½ cup unsweetened cocoa
1 cup boiling water
1½ cups sifted cake flour
1 teaspoon baking soda
¼ teaspoon baking powder
½ teaspoon salt
8 tablespoons (1 stick) unsalted
    butter, softened

1¼ cups granulated sugar
2 large eggs
2 teaspoons vanilla extract

Grandma's Fudge Frosting
    (page 198) or Chocolate Butter
    Frosting (page 197)

1. Position a rack in the center of the oven and preheat oven to 350°F. Grease and flour two 8-inch round cake pans.

2. Place the cocoa in a bowl and pour in the boiling water; stir to dissolve the cocoa and cool slightly.

3. In a medium-sized bowl stir together the cake flour, baking soda, baking powder, and salt.

4. In a large bowl with an electric mixer beat the butter until fluffy, about 1 minute, then gradually beat in the sugar. Beat in the eggs, one at a time; add the vanilla and beat until light and fluffy, 1 to 2 minutes. Beat in the dry ingredients alternately with the cocoa mixture, beginning and ending with dry ingredients. Divide batter between the prepared pans, smoothing the tops. Bake 25 to 30 minutes, until the tops spring back when lightly touched and a toothpick inserted in the center comes out with just a few crumbs clinging to it; do not overbake or the cakes will become too dry. Cool in the pans on a rack for 5 minutes. Run a knife around the edges to loosen from the pans and turn layers out on the rack, placing one upside down and the other right side up.

5. Brush any loose crumbs from the layers and place one upside down on a serving plate. Spread with about 1¼ cups of the frosting. Center the remaining layer, right side up, over the top. Frost the top and sides with the remaining frosting, making decorative swirls around the sides and over the top. Chill to set the frosting but return to room temperature before serving.

SILVER CAKE

This is a particularly fine white cake recipe,
combining a delicate texture and flavor with a beautiful white color.
It makes a very special birthday cake, and is ideally suited
for a many-layered wedding cake.

MAKES ONE 9-INCH 2-LAYER CAKE

2¾ cups sifted cake flour
1 tablespoon baking powder
½ teaspoon salt
8 tablespoons (1 stick) unsalted
   butter, softened
1½ cups granulated sugar
1 teaspoon vanilla extract

4 egg whites
1 cup milk

Chocolate Butter Frosting
   (page 197) or Old-fashioned
   Buttercream (page 196)

1. Position a rack in the center of the oven and preheat oven to 350°F. Grease and flour two 9-inch round cake pans, tapping out the excess flour.

2. In a medium-sized bowl sift together the flour, baking powder, and salt.

3. In a large bowl combine the butter and sugar and beat with an electric mixer until well combined. Add the vanilla and egg whites and beat at high speed until light, about 2 minutes. Beat in half of the dry ingredients, just until blended. Beat in all of the milk and then the remaining dry ingredients. Beat for one minute and then turn into the prepared pans, dividing batter equally between them. Smooth the tops with a spatula and firmly tap pans on the surface to level. Bake on same shelf until the tops spring back when lightly touched and a toothpick inserted in the center emerges clean, 30 to 35 minutes. Cool in the pans on a rack for 10 minutes and then invert onto racks. Return one layer to an upright position and cool both layers to room temperature.

4. Place one layer bottom side up on a serving dish and spread with 1 cup of

frosting. Add the second layer, right side up, over the frosting. Spread top and then sides with the remaining frosting.

GOLD CAKE

This recipe did not need one bit of adjusting—the sugar
and cake flour work exactly as they did when my grandmother made this cake
back in the 1930s. The layers are beautiful and level
and have a delicate crumb and flavor.

MAKES ONE 9-INCH 2-LAYER CAKE

2½ cups sifted cake flour
4 teaspoons baking powder
¼ teaspoon salt
12 tablespoons (1½ sticks)
   unsalted butter, softened
1¼ cups granulated sugar

8 egg yolks
1 teaspoon vanilla extract
¾ cup milk

Old-fashioned Buttercream
(page 196)

1. Position a rack in the center of the oven and preheat oven to 350°F. Grease and flour two 9-inch round cake pans.

2. In a medium-sized bowl, sift together the cake flour, baking powder, and salt.

3. In a large bowl, beat the butter with an electric mixer until fluffy. Gradually beat in the sugar and continue beating until blended. Add the egg yolks and vanilla and beat until light, 2 to 3 minutes. Working in batches, beat in the dry ingredients alternately with the milk. Turn into the prepared pans and bake about 35 minutes, until the tops spring back when lightly touched and a toothpick inserted in the center comes out clean. Cool in the pans on a rack for 5 minutes. Run a knife around the edges to loosen the cakes from the pans and turn out onto the rack, placing one layer right side up, to cool completely.

4. Place one layer, upside down, on a serving plate and spread with 1¼ cups of the buttercream. Center the remaining layer over it, right side up, and frost the top and sides with the remaining frosting. Refrigerate to set the frosting, but serve at room temperature.

AUNT CHARLOTTE'S MILK CHOCOLATE CAKE

Topped with creamy, chocolate butter frosting,
this tall old-fashioned layer cake was a great favorite at family gatherings,
especially our Sunday afternoon picnics. A slice of this cake, with a glass of cold
milk, is an irresistible treat.

MAKES ONE 9-INCH 2-LAYER CAKE

3 ounces (3 squares) semisweet
   chocolate
3 cups all-purpose flour
¾ teaspoon baking powder
½ teaspoon salt
8 tablespoons (1 stick) unsalted
   butter, softened
¼ cup vegetable shortening

2 cups granulated sugar
2 teaspoons vanilla extract
4 large eggs
1½ teaspoons baking soda
1½ tablespoons distilled white vinegar
1½ cups buttermilk

Chocolate Butter Frosting (page 197)

1. Position a rack in the center of the oven and preheat to 350°F. Lightly grease two 9-inch round cake pans. Fit the bottom of each with a round of waxed paper; grease the paper and then lightly flour the pans, tapping out the excess.

2. In the top of a double boiler over barely simmering water, melt the chocolate; scrape it into a small bowl to cool slightly until needed.

3. In a medium-sized bowl stir together the flour, baking powder, and salt.

4. In a large bowl combine the butter and shortening; with an electric mixer beat until fluffy, about 1 minute. Gradually beat in the sugar. Add the cooled chocolate and vanilla, beating until blended. Beat in the eggs, one at a time, and beat until light, 1 to 2 minutes.

5. In a small bowl combine the baking soda and vinegar, stirring briefly while it foams; stir in the buttermilk.

6. Beat one-third of the dry ingredients and then half of the buttermilk mixture into the butter mixture. Beat in half of the remaining dry ingredients and then the re-maining buttermilk mixture. Beat in the remaining dry ingredients, just until smooth. Divide batter between the prepared pans, smoothing the tops. Tap once or twice to level and bake about 45 minutes, until the tops spring back when lightly touched and a toothpick inserted in the center comes out clean. Cool in the pans on a rack for 10 minutes. Run a knife around the edges to loosen. Invert onto racks, turning one layer right side up, peel off the waxed paper, and cool to room temperature.

7. Place one layer upside down on a serving plate; spread with about 1 cup of the frosting. Invert the remaining layer over the frosting. Spread top and sides with the remaining frosting, swirling the frosting. Chill until set but serve at room temperature.

GERMAN CHOCOLATE CAKE

I often requested this cake for my birthday when I was young.
It is dramatically tall and delicious, and its three layers are sandwiched
with a rich, crunchy frosting filled with pecans and coconut.

MAKES ONE 9-INCH 3-LAYER CAKE

½ cup water
4 ounces (1 bar) German sweet
   chocolate, broken into squares
2¼ cups all-purpose flour
1 teaspoon baking soda
½ teaspoon salt

1 cup (2 sticks) unsalted butter, softened
1⅔ cups granulated sugar
4 large eggs
2 teaspoons vanilla extract
1 cup sour cream

Pecan-Coconut Frosting (page 202)

1. Evenly space two racks in the oven. Preheat to 350°F. Grease and flour three 9-inch round cake pans.

2. Bring ½ cup water to a simmer in a small saucepan; remove from heat. Add the chocolate and stir until smooth.

3. In a medium-sized bowl stir together the flour, baking soda, and salt.

4. In a large bowl combine the butter and sugar; beat with an electric mixer until light and fluffy, 2 to 3 minutes. Beat in the eggs, one at a time. Add the vanilla, sour cream, chocolate mixture, and flour; beat quickly, just until smooth. Turn the batter into the prepared pans, dividing it equally and smoothing the tops. Firmly tap each pan on a surface to level. Bake 35 to 40 minutes, until the tops spring back when lightly touched and a toothpick inserted in the center emerges clean. Cool in the pans for 10 minutes. Run a knife around the edges of the cakes and invert onto racks. Place one upside down and two right side up. Cool thoroughly.

5. Place one layer, bottom up, on a serving plate; spread with 1 cup of frosting. Center a second layer right side up over the frosting and cover with 1 cup more frosting. Add the final layer right side up and spread the remaining 1½ cups frosting over the top. Leave the sides unfrosted.

CARNIVAL CAKE

This luscious, festive cake is a guaranteed crowd-pleaser.
It is speckled with chocolate, moistened with a chunky nut filling,
and topped with swirling chocolate fudge frosting.

MAKES ONE 8-INCH 2-LAYER CAKE

2 cups all-purpose flour
½ cup packed dark brown sugar
½ cup granulated sugar
1 tablespoon baking powder
½ teaspoon baking soda
½ teaspoon salt
4 tablespoons (½ stick) unsalted
   butter, softened
¼ cup vegetable shortening

1¼ cups milk
3 large eggs
1½ teaspoons vanilla extract
6 ounces (6 squares) semisweet
   chocolate, chopped

Chocolate Butter Frosting (page 197) or
   Grandma's Fudge Frosting (page 198)

CARNIVAL NUT FILLING

6 tablespoons packed dark brown
   sugar
3 tablespoons all-purpose flour
¾ cup milk

3 tablespoons unsalted butter
¾ cup (3 ounces) chopped
   walnuts
2 teaspoons vanilla extract

1. Position a rack in the center of the oven and preheat oven to 350°F. Lightly grease the bottoms of two 8-by-1½-inch round layer-cake pans; line each with a round of waxed paper trimmed to fit and then grease the paper and the sides of the pans. Lightly flour, tapping out the excess.

2. In a large bowl stir together the flour, brown sugar, granulated sugar, baking powder, baking soda, and salt. Add the butter, vegetable shortening, milk, eggs, and vanilla; beat with an electric mixer on medium speed for 3 minutes, scraping the sides of the bowl occasionally, to make a thick, fluffy batter. Stir in the chopped chocolate. Divide the batter between the prepared pans, smoothing the tops. Drop each cake pan onto your work surface from a height of about 4 to 6 inches to level batter and remove air bubbles. Bake 35 to 45 minutes, until the tops spring back when lightly touched and a toothpick inserted in the center emerges clean. Cool in the pans on racks. Run a knife around the edges and invert the layers, peeling off and discarding the waxed paper.

3. While the cake is baking and cooling, prepare the filling. In a medium-sized heavy saucepan stir together the brown sugar and flour; stir in the milk until blended. Place over moderate heat and, stirring constantly, bring to a boil. Reduce the heat and simmer, stirring, for 3 minutes. Remove from the heat and stir in the butter, walnuts, and vanilla. Cover with waxed paper or plastic wrap placed directly on the surface, and cool to room temperature.

4. Brush the crumbs from the layers and place one, bottom up, on a serving plate. Spread all of the filling over the layer and top with the remaining layer, bottom down, With a spatula, frost the top and then the sides of the cake with 3 cups of the chocolate frosting. If desired, place any remaining frosting in a pastry bag fitted with a small star tip to pipe rosettes around the top, or reserve for another use. Let set for an hour or two before serving. If refrigerated, the icing will harden. Let soften to room temperature before serving.

HARVEST MOON CAKE

The romantic name of this tall layer cake conjures up images of the harvest moon during early fall. The colors are in keeping with the season. Like all cakes with seven-minute frostings, this one is best served on the day it is made.

MAKES ONE 8-INCH 3-LAYER CAKE

3 cups sifted cake flour
2½ teaspoons baking powder
½ teaspoon salt
8 tablespoons (1 stick) unsalted
   butter, softened
1½ cups packed dark brown sugar
2 large eggs

2 teaspoons vanilla extract
1⅓ cups milk
1 tablespoon dark rum (optional)
¼ cup (1 ounce) chopped walnuts
   or pecans

Seven-minute Caramel Frosting (page 201)

1. Evenly space two racks in the oven and preheat to 350°F. Grease and flour three 8-inch round cake pans.

2. In a medium-sized bowl stir together the flour, baking powder, and salt.

3. In a large bowl beat the butter with an electric mixer until fluffy. Gradually beat in the sugar. Beat in the eggs one at a time and then the vanilla, beating until light, 1 to 2 minutes. Beat in the milk alternately with the dry ingredients, beginning and ending with the dry ingredients. Turn the batter into the prepared pans, dividing it equally among them and leveling the batter with a spatula. Bake 25 to 30 minutes, until the tops spring back when lightly touched and a toothpick inserted in the center comes out clean. Cool in the pans on a rack for 5 minutes. Run a knife around the edges to loosen from the pans and turn the layers out on a rack to cool completely.

4. Place one layer right side up on a serving plate and brush with ½ tablespoon of the rum, if you wish. Spread with 1¼ cups frosting and top with a second layer, upside down; brush with ½ tablespoon of rum (optional) and spread with 1¼ cups frosting. Center the final layer upside down over the frosting and spread the top and sides with the remaining frosting, making swirls around the sides and over the top. Press the nuts around the top edge. Let set for an hour before serving.

PECAN LAYER CAKE

This beautiful layer cake gets its wonderful flavor from the freshly roasted pecans that go into the batter and decorate the edge of the frosted cake.

MAKES ONE 8-INCH 2-LAYER CAKE

1½ cups (6 ounces) pecan halves
8 tablespoons (1 stick) unsalted
   butter
2¼ cups all-purpose flour
¾ cup packed light brown sugar
½ cup granulated sugar
1 tablespoon baking powder

½ teaspoon salt
2 large eggs
1 cup milk
2 teaspoons vanilla extract

Old-fashioned Buttercream (page 196)

1. Position a rack in the center of the oven and preheat oven to 350°F. Scatter the pecans on a baking sheet and toast for about 12 minutes, turning them once or twice with a spatula. Cool completely. Reserve ½ cup of the best pecan halves and chop those remaining. Melt the butter in a small pan over low heat.

2. Grease and flour two 8-inch round cake pans.

3. In a large bowl stir together the flour, brown sugar, granulated sugar, baking powder, and salt.

4. In a medium-sized bowl whisk the eggs, milk, vanilla, and melted butter together. Pour over the dry ingredients and beat with an electric mixer for 1 to 2 minutes, until smooth and creamy. Stir in the chopped pecans and turn the batter into the prepared pans, dividing it equally between them and smoothing the tops. Bake 25 to 30 minutes, until the tops spring back when lightly touched and a toothpick inserted in the center comes out clean. Cool in the pans on a rack for 5 minutes. Run a knife around the edge to loosen the cakes from the pans and invert onto the rack to cool completely, turning one layer right side up.

5. Place one layer upside down on a serving plate and spread with 1¼ cups of buttercream. Center the remaining layer, right side up, over the buttercream and spread the top and sides with the remaining buttercream. Press the pecan halves around the side, near the top. Chill so the buttercream sets. Let come to room temperature for about 30 minutes before serving.

VERMONT MAPLE LAYER CAKE

Maple syrup could always be found in our house,
where we served it over my mother's special buttermilk pancakes. She also used
the syrup to make this beautifully delicate cake.

MAKES ONE 8-INCH 2-LAYER CAKE

2½ cups all-purpose flour
2 teaspoons baking powder
¾ teaspoon baking soda
½ teaspoon salt
¼ teaspoon ground cinnamon
4 tablespoons (½ stick) unsalted
    butter, softened
¼ cup vegetable shortening

½ cup granulated sugar
2 large eggs
1 cup pure Vermont maple syrup
2 teaspoons vanilla extract
½ cup water
½ cup (2 ounces) chopped walnuts

Fluffy Maple Frosting (page 201)

1. Position a rack in the center of the oven and preheat oven to 350°F. Grease and flour two 8-inch round cake pans.

2. In a medium-sized bowl stir together the flour, baking powder, baking soda, salt, and cinnamon.

3. In a large bowl combine the butter, shortening, and sugar; beat with an electric mixer until blended. Beat in the eggs, one at a time, beating until light, 1 to 2 minutes. Beat in the maple syrup in a steady stream, then beat in the vanilla. Working in batches, alternately beat in the dry ingredients with ½ cup water, starting and ending with dry ingredients. Turn into the prepared pans, smoothing the tops with a spatula, and bake 30 to 35 minutes, until the tops spring back when lightly touched and a toothpick inserted in the center comes out clean (the edges will have just started to pull away from the sides of the pan). Cool in the pans on a rack for 5 minutes; run a knife around the edges and turn out onto the rack to cool thoroughly, placing one layer right side up and the other upside down.

4. Place one layer, upside down, on a serving plate; spread with about 1 ½ cups of the freshly made frosting and sprinkle with ¼ cup of the walnuts. Top with the remaining layer, right side up, and frost the top and sides with the remaining frosting, swirling designs with a spatula around the sides. Sprinkle the remaining ¼ cup walnuts around the top edge. Let set for about 30 minutes. Serve at room temperature on the day the cake is made.

LEMON LAYER CAKE

Here is a cake with a light and delicate texture and a refreshingly tart lemon flavor. The buttercream is very lemony, too.

MAKES ONE 8-INCH 2-LAYER CAKE

2½ cups sifted cake flour
2 teaspoons baking powder
¼ teaspoon baking soda
¼ teaspoon salt
8 tablespoons (1 stick) unsalted
    butter, softened
2 teaspoons grated lemon zest

1¼ cups granulated sugar
2 large eggs
½ cup milk
½ cup fresh lemon juice

Lemon Buttercream (page 199)

1. Position a rack in the center of the oven and preheat to 375°F. Grease and flour two 8-inch round cake pans, tapping out the excess flour.

2. In a medium-sized bowl stir together the sifted cake flour, baking powder, baking soda, and salt.

3. In a large bowl combine the butter and lemon zest; with an electric mixer beat until fluffy. Gradually beat in the sugar. Beat in the eggs one at a time and then beat until light, 2 to 3 minutes. Beat in about one-fourth of the dry ingredients and then all of the milk. Beat in the remaining dry ingredients alternately with the lemon juice, beginning and ending with dry ingredients. Divide between the prepared pans and smooth the top of the batter with a spatula. Bake about 25 minutes, until the tops spring back when lightly touched and a toothpick inserted in the center comes out clean. Cool in the pans on a rack for 10 minutes. Run a knife around the edges to loosen from the pans and turn the layers out on a rack, turning one right side up. Cool to room temperature.

4. Place one layer upside down on a serving plate. Spread with 1 cup of the buttercream. Add the second layer right side up. Frost the top and sides with the remaining 2 cups of buttercream. Chill to set the frosting but serve at room temperature for best flavor.

1933 GLORY CAKE WITH PARADISE FILLING

A rainbow of flavors—lemon, apricot, banana, vanilla, and almond—mingle and marry in this unusual cake dating from 1933. The filling, a purée of apricots, bananas, and flavorings, is also used to frost the cake, although it is not really a frosting in the expected sense. Before you start the cake, put the dried apricots for the filling to soak, following instructions in Step 4. Then you can proceed with the filling while the cake is baking. Alternatively, you may make the filling well ahead of time.

MAKES ONE 8-INCH 3-LAYER CAKE

2⅓ cups all-purpose flour
2½ teaspoons baking powder
½ teaspoons salt
6 tablespoons (¾ stick) unsalted
    butter, softened
⅓ cup vegetable shortening

1⅓ cups granulated sugar
2 large eggs
1 teaspoon lemon extract
¾ cup milk
1½ cups (about 4½ ounces)
    shredded sweetened coconut

PARADISE FILLING

MAKES 4 CUPS

1 cup (8 ounces) packed dried
  apricots
1½ cups warm water
2 cups confectioner's sugar
2 tablespoons cornstarch

5 medium bananas (about
  2 pounds)
2 tablespoons lemon juice
2 teaspoons vanilla extract
¼ teaspoon almond extract

1. Position two racks in the center of the oven and preheat oven to 375°F. Grease and flour three 8-inch round cake pans.

2. In a medium-sized bowl stir together the flour, baking powder, and salt.

3. In a large bowl combine the butter and shortening; beat with an electric mixer until fluffy, about 30 seconds. Gradually add the sugar and beat until blended. Beat in the eggs one at a time, then add the lemon extract and beat until light, 1 to 2 minutes. Beat in the dry ingredients alternately with the milk, beginning and ending with dry ingredients. Divide the batter equally among the pans, smoothing the tops. Bake 20 to 25 minutes, until the tops spring back when lightly touched and the sides begin to pull away from the pans. Cool in the pans on a rack for 10 minutes and then turn out and cool the layers upside down on a rack.

4. While cake is baking and cooling, prepare filling. Place the apricots in a medium bowl, add 1½ cups very warm tap water and let soak for 1 hour. Transfer, undrained, to a heavy medium saucepan and bring to a boil over moderate heat. Reduce the heat slightly and simmer, stirring and mashing frequently, until thick as jam, 5 to 10 minutes. Cool slightly and then force through a sieve or purée in a food processor; return to the pan.

5. In a medium-sized bowl stir together the confectioner's sugar and cornstarch. Stir into the apricot purée until smooth and dissolved. Place over low heat and, stirring constantly, simmer for 5 minutes, until slightly thickened. Peel the bananas and thinly slice them directly into the purée. Cook, stirring constantly, for 5 minutes (if mixture should stick or scorch, immediately transfer it to another pot or to the top of a double boiler over simmering water). Remove from the heat and stir in the lemon juice, vanilla, and almond extract. Beat with an electric mixer until smooth, about 1 minute. Transfer to a bowl and cool to room temperature. If making ahead, cover and refrigerate. Return to room temperature before using to fill and frost cakes.

6. Working with all layers upside down, place one layer on a serving plate and spread with 1 cup of the filling. Center a second layer over the filling and spread with 1 cup of the filling. Top with the third layer. Spread top and sides with the remaining 2 cups of filling. Sprinkle the top with coconut and lightly press coconut to the sides all around. Chill. Return to room temperature before serving.

BANANA-PINEAPPLE CAKE

This cake, which my mother made often, is from a very old recipe
and has a medley of flavors—banana, pineapple, and cinnamon. The rich moist layers
are sandwiched with delicious cream cheese frosting. The cake slices well
and can be successfully refrigerated for a few days.

MAKES ONE 8-INCH 3-LAYER CAKE

3 cups all-purpose flour
1 teaspoon baking powder
½ teaspoon baking soda
1 teaspoon salt
1 teaspoon ground cinnamon
One 8-ounce can crushed
   pineapple in juice, undrained
2 cups (2 large) bananas,
   chopped in ¼-inch pieces
1½ cups granulated sugar

4 tablespoons (½ stick) unsalted
   butter, softened
1 cup vegetable oil
3 large eggs
2 teaspoons vanilla extract
1½ tablespoons rum or dry sherry
¾ cup (3 ounces) chopped walnuts

Cream Cheese Frosting (page 200)

1. Evenly space two racks in the oven and preheat to 350°F. Grease and flour three 8-inch round cake pans.

2. In a medium-sized bowl stir together the flour, baking powder, baking soda, salt, and cinnamon. In another medium-sized bowl toss together the undrained pineapple and chopped bananas.

3. In a large bowl combine the sugar and butter; beat with an electric mixer until blended. Beat in the oil until smooth and then add the eggs, one at a time, beating after each. Add the vanilla and beat until light, 1 to 2 minutes. With a spoon, stir in the dry ingredients and then the pineapple-banana mixture just until blended. Divide the batter equally among the prepared pans, smoothing the tops. Bake 30 to 35 minutes, until the tops spring back when lightly touched and a toothpick inserted in the center comes out clean. Cool in the pans on a rack for 10 minutes. Run a knife around each layer to separate them from the pans and invert the layers onto racks. Cool two right side up and one upside down.

4. Brush the crumbs from the layers and place one right side up on a serving plate. Brush the top with ½ tablespoon of the rum or sherry. Spread with ½ cup of frosting. Center the middle layer upside down over the frosting and brush with ½ tablespoon of the rum or sherry; spread with ½ cup of the frosting. Top with the last layer, right side up, and brush with the remaining ½ tablespoon of the rum. Frost the top and sides with the remaining 1⅔ cups frosting. Press the nuts around the sides of the cake and chill until the frosting has set. Serve at room temperature.

MARASCHINO CHERRY CAKE

The delicate pink layers of this very pretty cake are flecked with bits of red maraschino cherries and with finely chopped walnuts. On the original recipe card, which is now in my file, my mother noted that this was the first birthday cake she baked for my father, and it has remained one of his favorite cakes in all the years since.

MAKES ONE 8-INCH 2-LAYER CAKE

2½ cups all-purpose flour
1 cup granulated sugar
1 tablespoon baking powder
½ teaspoon salt
¾ cup milk
¼ cup juice from maraschino
   cherries
1 teaspoon vanilla extract
½ teaspoon almond extract

4 tablespoons (½ stick) unsalted
   butter, softened
¼ cup vegetable shortening
4 large egg whites
18 maraschino cherries, drained
   (save juice) and quartered
½ cup (2 ounces) chopped walnuts

Cream Cheese Frosting (page 200)

1. Position a rack in the center of the oven and preheat to 350°F. Grease two 8-inch round cake pans; line bottoms with rounds of waxed paper and then grease the paper.

2. In a large bowl stir together the flour, sugar, baking powder, and salt. In a small bowl stir together the milk and cherry juice; add to the flour mixture along with vanilla, almond extract, butter, and shortening. Beat with an electric mixer just until smooth. Add the egg whites and beat for 3 minutes at medium speed. With a spoon stir in the cherries and walnuts. Divide batter between the prepared cake pans, smoothing the tops. Firmly tap on a work surface to level. Bake about 30 minutes, until the tops spring back when lightly touched and a toothpick inserted in the center emerges clean. Cool in the pans on a rack for 10 minutes. Run a knife around the edge of the cakes to loosen them from the pans; invert onto racks and peel off waxed paper. Cool completely before frosting.

3. Brush away any crumbs from the cakes and place one layer, bottom side up, on a serving plate. Spread with ¾ cup of the frosting and center the remaining layer, bottom side down, over the frosting. Use remaining frosting to frost top and sides. Refrigerate until set. Return to room temperature before slicing and serving.

BOSTON CREAM PIE

A Boston cream pie is of course not a pie at all,
but a cake filled with pastry cream. Over the course of years it has also acquired
a chocolate frosting, as in this version. You'll find that this recipe makes a cake
greatly superior to those you may associate with bakeries
and traditional restaurant fare.

MAKES ONE 8-INCH 2-LAYER CAKE

1 cup sifted cake flour
1 teaspoon baking powder
¼ teaspoon salt
2 large eggs

¾ cup granulated sugar
1½ teaspoons vanilla extract
½ cup milk
2 tablespoons melted butter

FILLING

1 cup milk
⅓ cup granulated sugar
1 tablespoon all-purpose flour
1 tablespoon cornstarch

Pinch of salt
2 large egg yolks
2 tablespoons unsalted butter
1 teaspoon vanilla extract

FROSTING

3 tablespoons cold milk
1 ounce (1 square) unsweetened
  chocolate, chopped

1 teaspoon butter
1 cup sifted confectioner's sugar
¼ teaspoon vanilla extract

1. Position a rack in the center of the oven and preheat to 350°F. Butter the bottoms of two 8-inch round cake pans and fit each with a round of waxed paper. Do not butter the sides of the pans.

2. Prepare the cake: In a medium-sized bowl stir together the flour, baking powder, and salt.

3. Break the eggs into a medium-sized bowl and beat with an electric mixer until foamy and slightly thickened, about 1 minute. Gradually beat in the sugar. Beat in the vanilla. Add the dry ingredients and beat just until blended. Add the milk and melted butter and beat just until smooth. Turn the batter into the prepared pans, dividing it between them. Tap the pans firmly several times on your work surface to level batter and remove air bubbles. Bake about 20 minutes until the tops spring back when lightly touched and a toothpick inserted in the center comes out clean. Cool in the pans on a rack.

4. Prepare the filling: In a small heavy saucepan over moderate heat, scald the milk.

5. In a medium-sized bowl stir together the sugar, flour, cornstarch, and salt. Whisk in the hot milk in a steady stream until smooth. Transfer to a small heavy saucepan and cook over moderately low heat, stirring constantly, until the mixture thickens and comes to a boil. Simmer for a minute or two. Whisk the egg yolks in a medium bowl; whisking constantly, add the hot mixture and then pour it back into the small heavy saucepan. Simmer, stirring or whisking constantly, for 2 to 3 minutes more, until thickened. Remove from the heat and stir in the butter and vanilla. Turn into a shallow bowl, cover with plastic wrap or waxed paper placed directly on the surface, and cool completely.

6. Prepare the frosting: Put the milk in a small heavy saucepan and add the chocolate. Place over moderately low heat and stir until the chocolate has melted. Remove from the heat and stir in the butter. Gradually stir in the sugar and then the vanilla to make a smooth frosting. Chill, stirring frequently, until slightly stiffened and of a good spreading consistency.

7. Assemble the cake: Run a knife around the cakes to separate them from the pans. Invert and peel off the waxed paper. Place one layer upside down on a serving plate. Spread with the filling and top with the remaining layer, right side up. Spread the top with the chocolate frosting. Chill until set. After the frosting has set, the cake can be covered with plastic wrap and stored in the refrigerator. Cut into wedges to serve.

FINNISH TORTE

This makes a lovely dessert more akin to a cake than a torte.
The original recipe instructs: "Take a fruit juice glass that holds three eggs and measure the sugar and flour in the same glass." Since three large eggs measure about two-thirds of a cup, the calculations for the modern translation of this recipe were simple, and the cake worked perfectly.

MAKES ONE 9-INCH CAKE

⅔ cup all-purpose flour
1 teaspoon baking powder
Pinch of salt
3 large eggs
⅔ cup granulated sugar

1 teaspoon vanilla extract
¼ teaspoon almond extract

½ cup apricot jam

TOPPING

½ cup heavy cream
1 tablespoon confectioner's sugar

½ teaspoon vanilla extract

1. Position a rack in the center of the oven and preheat oven to 350°F. Butter and flour a 9-inch springform pan (or line a 9-inch cake pan bottom with waxed paper; grease and flour).

2. In a medium-sized bowl stir together the flour, baking powder, and salt.

3. In a large bowl beat the eggs with an electric mixer until frothy, about 1 minute. Gradually beat in the sugar and then the vanilla and almond extracts; add the dry ingredients and beat just until blended. Pour into the prepared pan and bake 20 to 25 minutes, until golden brown. When done, a toothpick inserted in the center will come out clean and the top, when lightly touched, will spring back. Cool in the pan on a rack.

4. Run a knife around the edge. Remove the sides of the pan and then use spatulas to transfer the cake from the pan bottom to a serving plate (or invert regular cake pan and peel off the waxed paper). With a long serrated knife, split the cake in two horizontally. Spread the apricot jam over the bottom half and replace the top.

5. In a small deep bowl (preferably chilled) whip the cream with chilled beaters until soft peaks form. Add the sugar and vanilla and beat just until stiff. Just before serving, spoon mounds of whipped cream around the top of the cake and in the center; or use a large star tip to pipe whipped cream rosettes.

MARBLE CAKE

This rich butter cake swirled with chocolate was one of my favorites as a child. Although we always frosted and served it from the pan, you might also turn it out and frost both top and sides with fudge frosting.

MAKES ONE 13-BY-9-INCH CAKE

3 ounces (3 squares) semisweet chocolate, chopped
2⅔ cups all-purpose flour
2½ teaspoons baking powder
1 teaspoon salt
8 tablespoons (1 stick) unsalted butter, softened

1½ cups granulated sugar
2 large eggs
1½ teaspoons vanilla extract
1¼ cups milk

Grandma's Fudge Frosting (page 198)

1. Position a rack in the center of the oven and preheat oven to 350°F. Grease and flour a 13-by-9-inch baking pan.

2. In the top of a double boiler over barely simmering water, melt the chocolate. Remove from the hot water and let cool slightly.

3. In a medium-sized bowl stir together the flour, baking powder, and salt.

4. In a large bowl beat the butter with an electric mixer until fluffy. Gradually beat in the sugar. Beat in the eggs one at a time, then the vanilla, beating until light, 1 to 2 minutes. Beat in the dry ingredients alternately with the milk, beginning and ending with dry ingredients.

5. Turn half of the batter into a medium-sized bowl and add the melted chocolate; fold together until the color is even. Spoon the plain batter and the chocolate batter alternately into the prepared pan to make a loose checkerboard pattern. Run a knife through the batter in several directions to create a marbled effect. Smooth the top and bake 35 to 40 minutes, until the top springs back when lightly touched and a toothpick inserted in the center comes out clean. Cool in the pan on a rack.

6. When cool, spread the top with the fudge frosting if you wish. Serve at room temperature.

COUNTRY APPLE CAKE

This tall cake is moist and full of freshly shredded apples.
Traditionally it is frosted with butterscotch buttercream, but I find it to be equally good with old-fashioned buttercream.

MAKES ONE 8-INCH 3-LAYER CAKE

3 cups all-purpose flour
2 teaspoons baking soda
½ teaspoon salt
2 teaspoons ground cinnamon
1 teaspoon freshly grated nutmeg
1 teaspoon ground ginger
1¼ cups granulated sugar
¾ cup vegetable oil
8 tablespoons (1 stick) unsalted butter, melted

2 large eggs
2 teaspoons vanilla extract
3 cups coarsely shredded peeled tart green apples (3 medium)
1 cup (4 ounces) chopped walnuts

Old-fashioned Buttercream (page 196) or Butterscotch Buttercream Frosting (page 199)

1. Adjust two racks in the oven so that they are evenly spaced. Preheat oven to 350°F. Grease three 8-inch round cake pans. Line bottoms with rounds of waxed paper; grease and flour, tapping out the excess flour.

2. In a medium-sized bowl stir together the flour, baking soda, salt, cinnamon, nutmeg, and ginger.

3. In a large bowl combine the sugar, vegetable oil, melted butter, eggs, and vanilla; beat until blended. Stir in the flour mixture and then the apples and walnuts. Divide the batter (it will be thick) among the three pans, smoothing the tops. Firmly tap them on a surface to level. Bake until the tops spring back when lightly touched and a toothpick inserted near the center emerges clean, 30 to 35 minutes. Cool in the pans on a rack for 10 minutes. Run a knife around the edges and invert onto racks and turn all right side up. Peel off paper and cool cakes completely.

4. Brush crumbs from cakes. Place one layer, right side up, on a serving plate. Spread with ¾ cup frosting. Add another layer and spread with ¾ cup frosting. Add the top layer. Use the remaining frosting to frost top and sides. Chill if desired.

APPLESAUCE CAKE

This was Grandma Wahlstrom's favorite applesauce cake,
moist and old-fashioned and fragrant with applesauce and spice. She would
sometimes decorate the finished cake by sifting confectioner's sugar evenly over
a lace doily placed on the cake's top; the doily would be carefully removed
to reveal an intricate sugar design on the surface of the cake.

MAKES ONE 13-BY-9-INCH CAKE

2 cups all-purpose flour
2 teaspoons baking soda
1 teaspoon baking powder
1½ teaspoons ground cinnamon
1 teaspoon freshly grated nutmeg
¼ teaspoon ground cloves
1 cup (6 ounces) raisins
1 cup (4 ounces) chopped
  walnuts

8 tablespoons (1 stick) unsalted
  butter, softened
1 cup granulated sugar
1 large egg
2 teaspoons vanilla extract
2 cups unsweetened applesauce
1 tablespoon confectioner's sugar
  for topping

1. Position a rack in the center of the oven and preheat to 350°F. Grease and flour a 13-by-9-inch baking pan.

2. In a medium-sized bowl stir together the flour, baking soda, baking powder, cinnamon, nutmeg, and cloves.

3. In a small bowl combine the raisins and walnuts; stir in ¼ cup of the flour mixture to coat.

4. In a large bowl, with an electric mixer, cream the butter until fluffy, about 1 minute. Add the sugar and beat until blended. Beat in the egg and vanilla. Beat in the dry ingredients, one-third at a time, alternating with the applesauce and beginning and ending with the dry ingredients. Stir in the reserved raisin and walnut mixture. Turn into the prepared pan and smooth the top. Bake 35 to 40 minutes, until the top springs back when lightly touched and a toothpick inserted in the center emerges clean. Cool in the pan on a rack.

5. If desired, place a lace doily on the top and sift the confectioner's sugar over it. Carefully remove doily, cut into squares, and serve.

CARROT CAKE

This cake was one of the later additions to the family recipe files,
and was for a number of years my mother's favorite cake recipe. Needless to say,
we contentedly ate carrot cake countless times
during a considerable part of my childhood.

MAKES ONE 13-BY-9-INCH CAKE

2½ cups all-purpose flour
1 teaspoon baking powder
1 teaspoon baking soda
1 teaspoon salt
2 teaspoons ground cinnamon
1 cup granulated sugar
½ cup packed light or dark
   brown sugar

4 tablespoons (½ stick) unsalted
   butter, softened
1 cup vegetable oil
5 large eggs
3 cups coarsely shredded peeled
   raw carrots (6 medium)
1½ cups (6 ounces) chopped walnuts

Cream Cheese Frosting (page 200)

1. Position a rack in the center of the oven and preheat to 350°F. Grease and flour a 13-by-9-inch baking pan.

2. In a medium-sized bowl stir together the flour, baking powder, baking soda, salt, and cinnamon.

3. In a large bowl combine the granulated sugar, brown sugar, and butter; beat with an electric mixer until evenly blended. Beat in the oil until smooth. Beat in the eggs, one at a time, and then beat until thick and light, 1 to 2 minutes. Add the dry ingredients and beat just until blended. With a spoon, stir in the shredded carrots and chopped walnuts; the batter will be thick. Turn the batter into the prepared pan, smoothing the top. Bake 50 to 60 minutes, until the top springs back when lightly touched and a toothpick inserted in the center comes out clean. Cool in the pan on a rack. When completely cool, generously frost, making swirls over the top. Cover and refrigerate. The frosting will set. To serve, return to room temperature and cut into squares.

MOM'S PINEAPPLE UPSIDE-DOWN CAKE

This cake is traditionally made with canned pineapple, but after she visited Hawaii my mother always made it with fresh pineapple. It's not easy to go back to canned pineapple once you've tasted this version.

MAKES ONE 9-INCH CAKE

1 medium-sized ripe pineapple
¾ cup granulated sugar
8 tablespoons (1 stick) unsalted
   butter
½ cup packed dark brown sugar
½ cup (2 ounces) chopped
   pecans or walnuts

2 large eggs, separated
1 teaspoon vanilla
⅓ cup milk
1 cup all-purpose flour
1 teaspoon baking powder

1. Trim the ends of the pineapple and cut off the tough outer skin. Remove the eyes. Cut 7 slices that are about ¾ inch thick and use a small round cutter to remove the core from each slice.

2. In a large enameled skillet or saucepan, combine ¼ cup of the granulated sugar with ½ cup of water; bring to a boil over moderate heat. Add enough pineapple slices to make one layer; poach, turning several times, for about 5 minutes, until tender. Remove slices to a plate to cool and repeat with the remaining slices. Drain pineapple on paper towels when cool. Discard any syrup remaining.

3. Position a rack in the center of the oven and preheat to 350°F. In a well-seasoned 10-inch cast-iron skillet, melt the butter. Remove 2 tablespoons and reserve in a small measuring cup. Add the brown sugar to the skillet and bring to a boil over moderately high heat, stirring. Boil for one minute without stirring and remove from the heat. Place one pineapple slice in the center and six around it. Distribute the pecans around the pineapple slices.

4. Place the egg whites in one medium-sized bowl and the yolks in another. Beat the whites until soft peaks just begin to form and gradually beat in ¼ cup of the remaining granulated sugar; continue beating until stiff glossy peaks form.

5. Add the remaining ¼ cup granulated sugar to the egg yolks and beat with an electric mixer until light, 1 to 2 minutes. Add the reserved 2 tablespoons melted butter, vanilla, and milk; beat just until blended. Add the flour and baking powder and beat just until smooth. With a large spoon, stir a large spoonful of the beaten whites into the batter to lighten it. Scrape all of the batter into the whites and quickly but thoroughly fold the two together. Pour batter carefully over the pineapple and nuts, and smooth the top. Bake about 30 minutes, until a toothpick inserted in the center emerges clean. Immediately invert a serving plate over the cake and unmold. Cool completely before serving.

Note: A 10-inch skillet is correct; the cake, when unmolded, will measure 9 inches in diameter because the bottom of a 10-inch skillet is 9 inches across.

GRANDMA'S BLACKBERRY CAKE

This very old-fashioned and distinctive cake is made with fresh blackberries. It has a sweet-tangy flavor and a rich marbleized color.

MAKES ONE 10-INCH BUNDT CAKE

1½ cups fresh blackberries
3 cups all-purpose flour
1½ cups granulated sugar
½ teaspoon salt
½ teaspoon ground cloves
¼ teaspoon ground cinnamon

12 tablespoons (1½ sticks)
   unsalted butter, melted
1 cup sour cream
3 large eggs
½ cup (2 ounces) finely chopped pecans
2 teaspoons baking powder
1 teaspoon baking soda

1. Position a rack in the center of the oven and preheat oven to 350°F. Butter and flour a 10-inch Bundt pan. Pick over the berries and rinse quickly only if they appear dirty.

2. In a large mixing bowl combine the flour, sugar, salt, cloves, and cinnamon; stir to blend. Add the melted butter, sour cream, and eggs. With an electric mixer, beat to moisten the ingredients. Add the blackberries and beat for one minute. Add the pecans, baking powder, and baking soda; beat just until blended. Quickly turn into the prepared pan and bake for 55 to 60 minutes, until the edges pull away from the sides of the pan and a toothpick inserted in the center emerges clean. Cool in the pan on a rack for 20 minutes and then invert onto a rack to cool completely.

GOLDEN CRUNCH CAKE

My grandmother once made this cake for my brother and me when we went to visit. The coconut topping, toasted under the broiler, produced such a delicious flavor and satisfying crunch that we ate the entire cake. My grandmother, undismayed, went back into the kitchen and made another.

MAKES ONE 8-INCH SQUARE CAKE

1 cup all-purpose flour
1 teaspoon baking powder
¼ teaspoon salt
2 large eggs
¾ cup granulated sugar

1 teaspoon vanilla extract
½ cup milk
2 tablespoons (¼ stick) unsalted butter, melted

TOPPING

4 tablespoons (½ stick) unsalted butter
¼ cup heavy cream
½ cup packed light brown sugar

½ cup (about 1½ ounces) shredded sweetened coconut
½ cup (2 ounces) chopped pecans or walnuts

1. Position a rack in the center of the oven and preheat oven to 350°F. Grease an 8-inch square pan. In a small bowl stir together the flour, baking powder, and salt.

2. In a medium-sized bowl beat the eggs with an electric mixer until they are foamy

and slightly thickened, about 1 minute. Gradually beat in the sugar and then the vanilla. Add the dry ingredients and beat just until moistened. Add the milk and melted butter and beat just until smooth. Turn the batter into the prepared pan. Bake about 25 minutes, until the top springs back when lightly touched and a toothpick inserted in the center emerges clean. Remove from the oven and increase the heat to broil.

3. To prepare the topping, combine the butter, cream, and brown sugar in a small saucepan. Place over moderate heat and stir until the butter is melted and the mixture is blended. Remove from the heat and stir in the coconut and nuts. Spoon the topping over the hot cake and broil until bubbly and golden brown, 1 to 2 minutes. Watch carefully; brown sugar burns easily. Cool in the pan on a rack. Serve warm or at room temperature, cut into squares.

OATMEAL CAKE WITH CRUNCHY OAT TOPPING

Moist, rich, and tasty, this simple cake may win you over completely—if, of course, you're in the mood for an old-fashioned cake with a crunchy oat and nut topping. This is comfort food at its best.

MAKES ONE 13-BY-9-INCH CAKE

1 cup old-fashioned rolled oats
1¼ cups boiling water
1½ cups all-purpose flour
1 teaspoon ground cinnamon
½ teaspoon baking powder
½ teaspoon baking soda
½ teaspoon salt

8 tablespoons (1 stick) unsalted butter, softened
¾ cup packed dark brown sugar
½ cup granulated sugar
2 large eggs
1 teaspoon vanilla extract

CRUNCHY OAT TOPPING

4 tablespoons (½ stick) unsalted butter
⅓ cup evaporated milk
½ cup packed dark brown sugar

½ cup old-fashioned rolled oats
½ cup (about 1½ ounces) sweetened shredded coconut
½ cup (2 ounces) chopped walnuts

1. Place the oats in a medium-sized heatproof bowl and pour the boiling water over them; stir once or twice and cool to lukewarm.

2. Position a rack in the center of the oven and preheat to 350°F. Grease a 13-by-9-inch baking pan.

3. In a medium-sized bowl stir together the flour, cinnamon, baking powder, baking soda, and salt.

4. In a large bowl with an electric mixer beat the butter until fluffy, about 1 minute. Gradually beat in the brown sugar and the granulated sugar. Beat in the eggs, one at a time, then the vanilla, and beat until light, 1 to 2 minutes. Add the dry ingredients and beat just until blended. With a spoon, stir in the oatmeal mixture. Turn the batter into the prepared pan, smooth the top, and bake about 35 minutes, until the top springs back when lightly touched and a toothpick inserted in the center comes out clean. Remove the cake from the oven and increase the heat to broil.

5. Meanwhile, prepare the topping: In a small saucepan combine the butter and evaporated milk; bring to a simmer and stir to melt the butter. Add the brown sugar and stir to dissolve. Remove from the heat and stir in the oats, coconut, and walnuts. Spread over the hot cake and place under the broiler for a minute or two, watching carefully, until bubbling and golden brown. Remove and cool in the pan on a rack. May be served just slightly warm if desired.

Mystery Cake of 1932

This is one of the few old recipes that can be precisely dated:
It was developed in 1932, during the worst of the Depression.
In keeping with the rather desperate circumstances of that time, it contains no eggs and very little butter. The rich, moist texture of the cake is most likely due to its use of tomato, a novel ingredient for a cake but perhaps not so surprising as it may seem—the tomato, after all, is technically a fruit.

MAKES ONE 13-BY-9-INCH CAKE

1½ cups all-purpose flour
1 teaspoon baking soda
1 teaspoon ground cinnamon
½ teaspoon freshly grated nutmeg
½ teaspoon ground cloves
¾ cup packed dark brown sugar

2 tablespoons unsalted butter, softened
One 10¾-ounce can tomato soup
1 cup (6 ounces) raisins, chopped
½ cup (2 ounces) chopped walnuts
1 tablespoon confectioner's sugar, for topping

1. Position a rack in the center of the oven and preheat to 350°F. Grease a 13-by-9-inch baking pan.

2. In a medium-sized bowl stir together the flour, baking soda, cinnamon, nutmeg, and cloves.

3. In another medium-sized bowl combine the brown sugar and butter; beat with an electric mixer until blended. Beat in the tomato soup until smooth. Stir in the raisins and walnuts. Turn the batter into the prepared pan, smoothing the top. Bake about 30 minutes, until the top springs back when lightly touched and a toothpick inserted in the center emerges clean. Cool in the pan, on a rack.

4. If desired, arrange on top of the cake ½-inch-wide strips of paper set on the diagonal in two directions to make a lattice pattern. Place the confectioner's sugar in a small sieve and sift over the paper. Carefully remove paper to reveal stenciled design. Cut into squares and serve.

AUNT MARIE'S SPICE CAKE

This addictively aromatic cake, with just the right amount of spice, has a slightly crunchy meringuelike topping.

MAKES ONE 9-INCH CAKE

4 tablespoons (½ stick) unsalted butter, at room temperature
¼ cup vegetable shortening
1¼ cups packed light brown sugar
2 large eggs
1⅓ cups sifted cake flour

½ teaspoon baking powder
½ teaspoon baking soda
½ teaspoon ground cinnamon
½ teaspoon ground cloves
¼ teaspoon salt
½ cup buttermilk
¼ cup (1 ounce) chopped walnuts

1. Position a rack in the center of the oven and preheat oven to 350°F. Lightly coat a 9-inch springform pan with shortening and dust with flour, tapping out the excess. In a large bowl, cream the butter and shortening together with an electric mixer or wooden spoon. Gradually beat in ¾ cup of the brown sugar. Separate one of the eggs and reserve the egg white for the topping. Add one whole egg and 1 egg yolk to the butter mixture and beat until blended.

2. Onto a sheet of waxed paper, sift together the flour, baking powder, baking soda, cinnamon, cloves, and salt. Add one-third of the dry ingredients and 2 tablespoons of the buttermilk to the butter mixture. Beat until just blended. Beat in half of the remaining dry ingredients and buttermilk. Beat in the remaining dry ingredients and buttermilk. Pour into the pan and tap to level the batter. Bake until a toothpick comes out clean when inserted in the center, about 35 minutes. Do not turn off oven.

3. In a medium-sized bowl, beat the reserved egg white until it forms stiff peaks. Crumble the remaining ½ cup brown sugar and gradually add it as you continue to beat to a glossy meringue. Spread the mixture over the top of the cake, sprinkle with walnuts, and bake until the topping is golden brown, about 15 minutes. Serve warm or at room temperature.

GRANDMA'S GINGERBREAD

Here is one of those wonderful old recipes
that can usually be prepared from ingredients on hand. How many times it was
simply thrown together after Sunday supper I can't even guess. But it's always
a welcome treat, with or without softly whipped cream.

MAKES ONE 11¾-BY-7½-INCH CAKE

2 cups all-purpose flour
1 teaspoon baking soda
1½ teaspoons ground ginger
1 teaspoon ground cinnamon
¼ teaspoon ground cloves
½ teaspoon salt

5 tablespoons unsalted butter, softened
⅓ cup honey
1 large egg
⅔ cup dark molasses
¾ cup milk
Heavy cream, whipped soft, for
    topping (optional)

1. Position a rack in the center of the oven and preheat to 350°F. Grease an 11¾-by-7½-inch baking dish.

2. In a medium-sized bowl stir together the flour, baking soda, ginger, cinnamon, cloves, and salt.

3. In a large bowl with an electric mixer, cream the butter. Gradually beat in the honey. Add the egg and beat until fluffy. Add the molasses and beat until well blended. With a spoon, stir in the dry ingredients alternately with the milk, beginning and ending with dry ingredients. Turn batter into the prepared pan, smoothing the top. Bake 30 to 35 minutes, until the top springs back when lightly touched and a toothpick inserted near the center emerges clean. Cool in the pan on a rack for about 15 minutes. Cut into squares and serve warm, with whipped cream if you wish.

POPPYSEED CAKE

Aunt Charlotte made this cake often, adjusting and developing the recipe over the years until its rich, moist interior entirely satisfied her. It is made in a tube or bundt pan, and is particularly good for picnics or luncheons.

MAKES ONE 10-INCH TUBE CAKE

POPPYSEED FILLING

¾ cup (4 ounces) whole
  poppyseeds

⅔ cup milk
¼ cup granulated sugar

CAKE

One 12-ounce can evaporated milk
1 cup (4 ounces) chopped walnuts
3 cups all-purpose flour
1½ teaspoons baking soda
½ teaspoon salt

4 large eggs
1¾ cups granulated sugar
1 cup vegetable oil
2 teaspoons vanilla extract
1 tablespoon confectioner's sugar

1. First, make the filling: Combine the poppyseeds and milk in a blender container; blend to grind seeds. Transfer to a small heavy saucepan and stir in the sugar. Place over moderate heat and, stirring constantly, cook until as thick as muffin batter, 5 to 10 minutes. Cool to room temperature. This filling can be made a day or two ahead of time and stored, covered, in the refrigerator.

2. Position a rack in the lower half of the oven and preheat to 350°F. Have ready an ungreased 10-inch tube pan with a removable bottom.

3. Place the poppyseed filling in a medium-sized bowl and gradually stir in the evaporated milk, then the walnuts.

4. In another medium-sized bowl, stir together the flour, baking soda, and salt.

5. In a large bowl combine the eggs, sugar, vegetable oil, and vanilla; beat with an electric mixer until light, 2 to 3 minutes. Beat in the poppyseed mixture until blended. Add the dry ingredients and beat just until evenly blended. Turn into the ungreased tube pan and bake for 1 hour to 1 hour and 15 minutes, or until a toothpick inserted in the center comes out clean and the top springs back when lightly touched. Cool completely in the pan, right side up, on a rack. Run a knife around the sides to separate, then remove the pan sides. Run a knife under the bottom of the cake and around the inner tube to separate, and remove the pan bottom. Place the cake on a serving dish, right side up, and sift the top with the confectioner's sugar. Cut into thin slices and serve.

POUND CAKE

Pound cake derives its name from the original formula
from which it was made: one pound each of butter, sugar, flour, and eggs,
enough to make two loaves. This old recipe of Aunt Irma's calls for approximately
one-half pound of each of the ingredients and yields one loaf.

MAKES ONE 9-BY-5-INCH LOAF

2 cups all-purpose flour
½ teaspoon baking powder
½ teaspoon salt
1 cup (2 sticks) unsalted butter,
    softened

1 cup granulated sugar
5 large eggs, at room temperature
2 teaspoons vanilla extract

1. Position a rack in the center of the oven and preheat oven to 325°F. Grease and flour a 9-by-5-by-3-inch loaf pan.

2. In a medium-sized bowl stir together the flour, baking powder, and salt.

3. In a large bowl beat the butter with an electric mixer until fluffy. Gradually beat in the sugar until blended. One at a time, beat in the eggs, and then add the vanilla. Add the dry ingredients and beat just until smooth. Turn into the prepared pan and bake until the top peaks and turns golden brown, about 1 hour and 15 minutes; when cake is done the top will spring back when lightly touched and a toothpick inserted in the center will come out clean. Cool in the pan on a rack for 10 minutes; turn out and cool thoroughly on a rack. Slice and serve.

ORANGE FLUFF CAKE

The orange trees in the backyard of our house in California, where we moved in the early 1950s, afforded us a constant supply of fresh, juicy oranges for this lovely cake.

MAKES ONE 10-INCH TUBE CAKE

1½ cups sifted cake flour
1 cup granulated sugar
2 teaspoons baking powder
½ teaspoon salt
5 tablespoons unsalted butter, melted

1 teaspoon grated orange zest
⅓ cup strained fresh orange juice
6 large eggs, separated
1 teaspoon vanilla extract
½ teaspoon cream of tartar

GLAZE

1 cup sifted confectioner's sugar
1 teaspoon grated orange zest

2 tablespoons fresh orange juice

1. Position a rack in the center of the oven and preheat to 350°F. Have ready an ungreased 10-inch tube cake pan with a removable bottom. (Do not use a tube pan with a nonstick surface.)

2. Sift the flour, ½ cup sugar, the baking powder, and salt into a medium-sized bowl. Form a well in the center and add the melted butter, orange zest, orange juice, egg yolks, and vanilla. With an electric mixer, beat until smooth, 1 to 2 minutes.

3. In a large bowl combine the egg whites and cream of tartar; beat with an electric mixer until soft peaks begin to form. Gradually beat in the remaining ½ cup sugar and continue to beat until stiff glossy peaks form. Stir a large spoonful of the whites into the batter to lighten. With a spatula, quickly fold in the remaining egg whites, half at a time, to make a fluffy batter that is even in color. Turn into the ungreased tube pan and bake 1 hour to 1 hour and 15 minutes, until the top springs back when lightly touched and a toothpick inserted emerges without crumbs clinging to it. Immediately invert and let the cake hang upside down until completely cool. (If the pan does not have tabs on its rim, place tube over the neck of a bottle.) Turn right side up and run a sharp knife around the edge to separate the cake from the pan. Remove sides. Run a knife around the center tube and under the cake; remove the pan bottom. Turn the cake right side up on a serving plate.

4. Prepare glaze: In a small bowl combine the confectioner's sugar, orange zest, and orange juice to make a glaze. Spread over the top of the cake, letting some drip down the sides. Let stand at room temperature until glaze has set, about 1 hour.

GRANDMA WAHLSTROM'S SPONGE CAKE

This wonderful old recipe, which dates back to the 1930s, was often topped with fresh berries during the summer. However you decide to serve it, plain or with fruit and perhaps whipped cream, it is a lovely light and fluffy cake.

MAKES ONE 10-INCH TUBE CAKE

6 large eggs, separated
¼ teaspoon cream of tartar
1¼ cups superfine sugar, sifted

½ teaspoon almond extract
½ teaspoon vanilla extract
1 cup sifted cake flour

1. Position a rack in the center of the oven and preheat to 350°F. Place the egg yolks in a medium-sized bowl and the whites in a large bowl; cover them and let them come to room temperature. Have ready an ungreased 10-inch tube pan with a removable bottom. (Do *not* use one with a nonstick surface.)

2. Add the cream of tartar to the egg whites and beat with an electric mixer until soft peaks just begin to form. Gradually beat in 1 cup of the sugar and continue to beat until stiff, glossy peaks form. Do not overbeat.

3. Beat the remaining ¼ cup sugar into the egg yolks. Add the almond extract and the vanilla; beat for 2 minutes. With a spatula, fold the egg yolk mixture into the whites. Sift one-fourth of the flour over the eggs and quickly but thoroughly fold them together. Repeat with the remaining flour, one-fourth at a time. Turn into the ungreased pan. Bake 40 to 50 minutes, until the top springs back when lightly touched; a toothpick inserted in the center will emerge clean. When done, remove from the oven and turn upside down; if your pan does not have legs to support it upside down, invert it over the neck of a bottle and let hang until cool. Turn right side up and run a knife around the edge to separate the cake from the pan. Remove sides and run a knife under the cake and around the tube. Remove cake and place right side up on a serving plate. Slice with a serrated knife.

AUNT MARIE'S ANGEL FOOD CAKE

This is the formula Aunt Marie used to make her special cloudlike angel food cake. It is best served on the day it is made.

MAKES ONE 10-INCH TUBE CAKE

1 ½ cups egg whites (about 12 large)
1 cup sifted cake flour
1 ¼ cups superfine sugar

½ teaspoon salt
1 teaspoon cream of tartar
2 teaspoons vanilla extract
2 teaspoons warm water

1. Position a rack in the lower half of the oven and preheat to 350°F. Have ready an ungreased 10-inch tube pan with a removable bottom (do not use one with a nonstick surface).

2. Let the egg whites come to room temperature and make sure that there is not one speck of yolk mixed in with them or they will not whip up properly. To remove an accidental speck of yolk, dab it with a small piece of bread; the yolk speck will cling to the bread.

3. Sift the flour and ¼ cup of the sugar onto a sheet of waxed paper. Working back and forth between that and another sheet of waxed paper, sift the mixture three times. Have the remaining 1 cup sugar measured and within arm's reach.

4. In a large bowl combine the egg whites with the salt, cream of tartar, vanilla, and warm water; with an electric mixer beat at high speed until soft peaks just begin to form. With the speed set at moderately low, gradually beat in the 1 cup sugar, beating in about 1 tablespoon at a time. When all sugar has been added, increase the speed to high and beat until stiff, glossy peaks form. Do not overbeat. Sift one-sixth of the flour-sugar mixture over the meringue and, with a large spatula, quickly and carefully fold in. Quickly fold in the remaining flour-sugar mixture one-sixth at a time in the same manner. Turn into the ungreased tube pan. Run a knife directly down the middle all around to help it rise properly. Bake 40 to 45 minutes, until a long skewer inserted in the middle emerges clean; the top will spring back when lightly touched and the top edge will have just begun to pull away from the pan. When done, remove from the oven and turn upside down; if your pan does not have legs to support it upside down, invert it over the neck of a bottle and let hang until cool, about 1 ½ hours. Turn right side up and run a knife around the edge to separate the cake from the pan. Remove sides and run a knife under the cake and around the tube. Remove cake and place right side up on a serving plate.

5. To serve the cake, portions can be pulled apart with two forks, held back to back, or you can use an angel food cake comb. You can also use a good serrated knife.

AFTERNOON TEA CAKES

This was a favorite recipe of my Aunt Marie's.
The light and moist cupcakes have a delicate cinnamon-scented chocolate glaze that's spread over them while they are still warm.

MAKES 1 DOZEN 2½-INCH CUPCAKES

3 tablespoons unsweetened cocoa powder
½ cup hot water
3 tablespoons unsalted butter, melted
¾ cup granulated sugar
1 large egg
½ cup sour cream

1 teaspoon baking soda
1 cup all-purpose flour
1 teaspoon vanilla extract
⅓ cup (about 1 ounce) sweetened shredded coconut

Chocolate Glaze (page 203)

1. Position a rack in the center of the oven and preheat to 375°F. Line twelve 2½-inch muffin cups with paper liners.

2. Place the cocoa in a small bowl and stir in ½ cup very hot tap water to dissolve.

3. In a large bowl combine the melted butter and sugar; beat with an electric mixer until blended. Add the egg and beat until light, 1 to 2 minutes. Add the cocoa mixture and beat until smooth. In a small bowl stir together the sour cream and baking soda. Stir this mixture into the butter-sugar mixture. Add the flour and vanilla; beat quickly, just until evenly blended. With a spoon stir in the coconut. Spoon the batter into the muffin cups, dividing it equally among them; they will be about three-quarters full. Bake about 20 minutes, until the tops spring back when lightly touched and a toothpick inserted in the center comes out clean. Remove the tea cakes from the pan and cool slightly on a rack while you prepare the glaze.

4. Spread about 2 teaspoons of the chocolate glaze on each of the warm tea cakes and let cool thoroughly.

MOM'S JELLY ROLL

This was one of my favorite desserts when I was a child. I loved the pretty red spiral made by my mother's homemade strawberry jam as it soaked into the delicate yellow spongecake. It is equally delicious made with raspberry or blackberry jam.

MAKES ONE 15-INCH ROLL

2 tablespoons unsalted butter	½ teaspoon salt
⅔ cup all-purpose flour	½ cup granulated sugar
½ teaspoon baking powder	3 tablespoons confectioner's sugar
5 large eggs, separated	One 12-ounce jar strawberry,
1 teaspoon vanilla extract	raspberry, or blackberry jam or jelly

1. Position a rack in the center of the oven and preheat to 400°F. Lightly grease a 17-by-11-inch jelly roll pan. Line with waxed paper and grease and lightly flour the paper.

2. Melt the butter in a small pan and let it cool slightly. In a medium-sized bowl, stir together the flour and baking powder.

3. In a small bowl stir together the egg yolks and vanilla; stir in half of the dry ingredients.

4. In a large, deep bowl combine the egg whites and salt; with an electric mixer, beat until soft peaks just begin to form. Gradually beat in the granulated sugar and continue to beat just until stiff, glossy peaks form.

5. Fold about one-fourth (or a large spoonful) of the egg whites into the yolk mixture to lighten. Turn this mixture into the bowl of whites and partially fold together. Sift the remaining dry ingredients over the top; quickly and gently but thoroughly fold together with a spatula until no streaks remain. Quickly spread the batter in the prepared pan and bake 8 to 10 minutes, or just until the top springs back when lightly touched.

6. Sift 2 tablespoons of the confectioner's sugar onto a clean kitchen towel. Invert the cake onto it and peel off the paper (if it has stuck or is stubborn, lightly brush the paper with water before peeling off). With a sharp knife, trim off about ½ inch from all four edges. Starting with one long side, roll up, jelly roll fashion. Wrap in the towel and cool to room temperature.

7. Carefully unroll the cake onto a board. Spread with the jelly or jam. Reroll, placing cake seam side down, and sift the remaining 1 tablespoon of confectioner's sugar over the top. Let rest about 1 hour before serving. Cut into slices and serve at room temperature.

CHOCOLATE COFFEE CREAM ROLL

Rich and delectable, this showy dessert makes an elegant finale to any dinner. The coffee and cream flavors are the perfect complement to the chocolate sponge roll.

MAKES ONE 15-INCH ROLL

2 tablespoons unsalted butter
½ cup all-purpose flour
⅓ cup plus 2 tablespoons
   unsweetened cocoa
½ teaspoon baking powder

5 large eggs, separated
¾ cup granuated sugar
1 teaspoon vanilla extract
½ teaspoon salt

COFFEE CREAM FILLING

1½ cups milk
1 tablespoon cold water
1 teaspoon unflavored gelatin
½ cup granulated sugar
¼ cup all-purpose flour

¼ teaspoon salt
3 egg yolks
2 tablespoons instant coffee powder
1 teaspoon vanilla extract
1 cup heavy cream

1. Position a rack in the center of the oven and preheat to 400°F. Lightly grease a 17-by-11-inch jelly roll pan. Line with waxed paper and grease and lightly flour the paper.

2. Prepare the chocolate roll. Melt the butter in a small pan and let it cool slightly. In a medium-sized bowl stir together the flour, ⅓ cup of the cocoa, and the baking powder.

3. In another medium-sized bowl whisk together the 5 egg yolks, ¼ cup of the sugar, and the melted butter until light, about 1 minute. Whisk in the vanilla. With a spoon, stir in about half of the dry ingredients.

4. In a large, deep bowl combine the egg whites and salt; with an electric mixer, beat until soft peaks just begin to form. Gradually beat in the remaining ½ cup sugar, beating just until stiff, glossy peaks form.

5. Fold about one-fourth (or a large spoonful) of the egg whites into the egg yolk mixture to lighten. Turn this mixture into the bowl of egg whites and partially fold together. Sift the remaining dry ingredients over the top and quickly and gently but thoroughly fold together until no streaks remain. Quickly spread in the prepared pan and bake 10 to 12 minutes, just until the center top springs back when lightly touched.

6. Sift the remaining 2 tablespoons of cocoa onto a clean kitchen towel. Invert the cake onto it and peel off the paper (if it has stuck or is stubborn, lightly brush the paper with water before peeling off). With a long, sharp knife or a serrated knife, trim away about ½ inch from each edge. Starting along one long side, roll up, jelly roll fashion. Wrap in the towel and let cool to room temperature.

7. While roll cools, prepare the coffee cream. In a medium-sized saucepan over low heat, scald the milk until tiny bubbles appear around the edges of the surface. Place 1 tablespoon cold water in a cup and sprinkle the gelatin over it. Let soften until needed.

8. In a medium-sized bowl stir together the sugar, flour, and salt. Gradually whisk in the scalded milk. Place in a heavy medium-sized saucepan over moderately low heat and, stirring constantly, cook until the mixture thickens and comes to a simmer. Whisk in the egg yolks and continue cooking and stirring until the mixture comes to a boil. Remove from the heat and stir in the coffee powder and dissolved gelatin until smooth; stir in the vanilla. Turn into a shallow bowl, cover with plastic wrap or waxed paper placed directly on the surface, and cool just to room temperature.

9. Assemble the roll. Using chilled bowl and beaters, whip the cream until stiff. Give the coffee cream filling a good stir and fold in about one-fourth of the whipped cream to lighten. Turn the lightened coffee filling into the whipped cream and fold together.

10. Carefully unroll the chocolate cake onto a board. Spread all of the coffee cream over it, making it thicker along the long side where you will begin to reroll and leaving about 1 inch uncoated along the other long side. Reroll the chocolate cake to enclose the filling. Leave it on the board, seam side down, cover, and chill until set, at least 4 hours or overnight. Trim the ends and cut into slices. Serve cold.

BURNT BUTTER CUPCAKES

The rich, sweet taste of the browned butter
in these cupcakes may not be as familiar now as when I was a boy, but if you try
this recipe you'll find that the cupcakes are very good indeed. You may also
make this recipe as a layer cake.

MAKES 2 DOZEN 2½-INCH CUPCAKES

8 tablespoons (1 stick) unsalted
   butter
2¼ cups all-purpose flour
2½ teaspoons baking powder
½ teaspoon salt
¼ cup vegetable shortening
1¼ cups granulated sugar
3 large eggs

2 teaspoons vanilla extract
¾ cup milk
24 pecan halves

Burnt Butter Glaze (page 202) or
   Fluffy Burnt Butter Frosting
   (page 197)

1. Place the butter in a small heavy skillet over moderate heat; melt, stirring frequently, and cook until deep brown, about 3 minutes. Pour into a small bowl, cool to room temperature, cover, and chill until solid. Soften to room temperature before proceeding.

2. Position a rack in the center of the oven and preheat to 350°F. Line 2 dozen 2½-inch muffin cups with paper liners.

3. In a medium-sized bowl stir together the flour, baking powder, and salt.

4. In a large bowl combine the shortening with the softened burnt butter; beat with an electric mixer until fluffy. Gradually beat in the sugar until blended. Beat in the eggs, one at a time, then the vanilla, and beat until light, 1 to 2 minutes. Add the dry ingredients alternately with the milk, beginning and ending with dry ingredients. Spoon the batter into the paper-lined muffin cups, filling them about two-thirds full. Bake until the tops spring back when lightly touched, about 25 minutes. Remove cupcakes from the pan and cool on a rack. If using the glaze, spread 2 teaspoons over each while the cupcakes are still very warm, so glaze remains shiny. If using the frosting, spread 4 teaspoons of frosting over each top after they have cooled completely. Center a pecan half over each cupcake immediately after glazing or frosting.

GOLDEN FRUITCAKE

A festive cake with a beautiful golden color
and a rich, moist interior filled with candied cherries and pineapple and with
apricots, walnuts, and raisins. The top may be decorated with more candied fruits,
if you wish. Make the cake four to six weeks before you plan to serve it,
so that the flavors have time to mature.

MAKES ONE 10-INCH TUBE CAKE (7 POUNDS)

1 pound (2 cups) candied whole red cherries
1 pound (2 cups) candied pineapple, cut into 1-inch pieces
8 ounces (1 cup) candied mixed citrus peel, chopped
8 ounces (1 cup) dried apricots, quartered
1 cup (6 ounces) golden raisins
1 cup brandy
1 tablespoon vanilla extract
2 cups (8 ounces) coarsely chopped walnuts
2 teaspoons grated fresh lemon zest

2 cups all-purpose flour
1 teaspoon baking powder
½ teaspoon baking soda
½ teaspoon salt
1½ teaspoons ground cinnamon
1 teaspoon freshly grated nutmeg
1 cup (2 sticks) unsalted butter, softened
¾ cup packed light brown sugar
½ cup dark corn syrup
6 large eggs
¼ cup fresh lemon juice
Light corn syrup and candied fruit for garnish (optional)

1. In a large bowl combine the cherries, pineapple, citrus peel, apricots, raisins, brandy, and vanilla; toss together, cover, and let stand at room temperature 12 hours or overnight, stirring occasionally. The liquid will be absorbed. Stir in the walnuts and lemon zest.

2. Grease a 10-inch tube pan. Cut pieces of smooth brown wrapping paper to fit the bottom and sides of the pan. Line pan with paper and grease the paper.

3. Adjust a rack to the lower half of the oven. Place a shallow pan of hot water on the oven floor and preheat the oven to 250°F. In a medium-sized bowl stir together the flour, baking powder, baking soda, salt, cinnamon, and nutmeg.

4. In a large bowl beat the butter with an electric mixer until fluffy, about 1 minute. Gradually beat in the brown sugar and then the corn syrup. Beat in the eggs, one at a time. Beat in one-third of the dry ingredients and then the lemon juice. Beat in the remaining dry ingredients, half at a time. It doesn't matter if the batter "breaks." Give the candied fruits a final stir, turn the mixture into the batter and stir until evenly blended. You will have 12 cups of batter. Turn the batter into the prepared pan, packing it firmly and smoothing the top. Bake 3 to 3½ hours, until golden brown; a toothpick inserted in the center will come out clean and the top will spring back when lightly touched. Cool in the pan on a rack, 6 hours or more.

5. Carefully remove the cake from the pan but leave the paper attached to the cake. With scissors, trim the paper even with the top of the cake. Enclose in plastic wrap and seal tightly in a covered container. Store in a cool place for 1 month. It is a good idea to check the cake after a week. If it seems dry, wrap in cheesecloth that has been sprinkled with brandy, rewrap in plastic wrap, and return to the container.

6. If you wish to decorate the top of the cake, peel off the paper. Brush the top with corn syrup and apply a decoration of candied fruit over the top. Brush with corn syrup.

7. Refrigerate the cake overnight for easier slicing. With a sharp knife, cut into thin slices.

❧ PIES ❧

My mother made the best peach pie I have ever tasted, for which she used only our own giant tree-ripened Elberta peaches. She'd drop a few peaches at a time into a big enameled kettle filled with boiling water, then rinse them under cold tap water before peeling and slicing them. She'd roll out the pie dough on our big mahogany dining room table, then roll and cut a second piece of pastry into strips to be woven into a lattice atop the sliced peaches. The top would be brushed with egg yolk and sprinkled with sugar before the pie went into the oven. As it baked, the pie would fill the house with an indescribably wonderful aroma, emerging from the oven all juicy and bubbly and golden. We would wait for what seemed like forever while the finished pie cooled on the windowsill, then eat it ever so slightly warm, plain or with ice cream.

It is often said that cooks may be judged by the quality of their pies. But although it may seem a bit daunting to produce a beautifully crisp and flaky crust, in fact it is a very easy matter if you follow a few simple rules. It is best to work with cold ingredients that are never allowed to become warm; so if you are at all apprehensive about making pie pastry, chill the shortening, flour, pastry blender, bowl, and board before you begin. If your hands tend to be warm, you may want to run cold water over them or rub them with ice cubes before working with the pastry. In practice, I never bother with any of these measures: if you are very quick at putting the pastry together, you'll find that they are not necessary.

Once you have quickly blended the ingredients, gather the pastry into a flat round and chill it. After rolling it out, you can chill it again before lining the pie pan, and keep the pastry-lined pan in the refrigerator until baking time. The general rule is to chill the pastry thoroughly any time it has had a chance of becoming warm, and then to pop it into a very hot oven. If you follow this general procedure along with the specific instructions in the recipe you have chosen, you will turn out a perfect pie crust every time.

GLAZED STRAWBERRY PIE

Our family enjoyed this pie more often than any other for
several reasons: (1) We love it, (2) strawberries are plentiful and cheap during
much of the summer, and (3) it's simple and colorful, adding a festive touch
to innumerable family picnics and parties.

MAKES ONE 9-INCH PIE

4 pints ripe strawberries
2 tablespoons water
⅔ cup granulated sugar
2 tablespoons cornstarch
1 tablespoon lemon juice

1 teaspoon vanilla extract

1 Cookie Crumb Shell (page 91)
or other baked shell

1. Quickly rinse the strawberries and hull them. Select 3 pints of the best-looking berries for the shell and drain them on paper towels. Use the remaining 1 pint for the glaze.

2. Using a paring knife, cut the berries reserved for the glaze into quarters and place them in a heavy medium-sized saucepan. Add 2 tablespoons of water and place over moderately high heat. Mashing with a fork or a potato masher, bring the mixture to a boil. Cook, stirring frequently, until very juicy, about 2 minutes. Place a sieve over a bowl and force the berries through, discarding any solids that remain. Measure the juice; you should have 1 cup. If there is less, add water to make 1 cup. If there is more, reserve the excess for another use.

3. On a sheet of waxed paper, combine the sugar and the cornstarch, mixing them together with your fingers. Place the strawberry juice in a heavy medium-sized saucepan, and gradually whisk in the sugar-cornstarch mixture until smooth. Add the lemon juice and cook over moderate heat, stirring constantly, until the mixture thickens and boils. Boil for a minute or two, until translucent. Remove from the heat and stir in the vanilla.

4. Arrange one-third of the well-drained strawberries in the shell and drizzle with one-third of the hot glaze. Repeat 2 more times with the remaining berries and glaze. Chill until set, 2 to 3 hours. Serve cold.

GLAZED BLUEBERRY PIE

My mother made this simple pie as soon as the first blueberries
of the season came to market. In a crisp cookie crumb shell, vanilla pastry cream
is layered with lots of fresh blueberries, which are topped by a shimmering
glaze flavored with orange zest.

MAKES ONE 9-INCH PIE

PASTRY CREAM

¼ cup granulated sugar
3 tablespoons all-purpose flour
Pinch of salt
1 cup half and half, light cream,
   or milk

3 egg yolks
3 tablespoons unsalted butter
1 teaspoon vanilla extract

FILLING

1 tablespoon confectioner's sugar
3 pints fresh blueberries
⅔ cup granulated sugar
1 tablespoon cornstarch
1½ teaspoons minced or grated
   orange zest

1 Cookie Crumb Shell (page 91)
   or other baked shell

1. Make the pastry cream: In a heavy medium-sized saucepan combine the sugar
and flour, stirring until thoroughly mixed. Add a pinch of salt and gradually whisk
in the cream or milk. Stirring or whisking constantly, cook over moderate heat until
as thick as medium white sauce.

2. Place the egg yolks in a small bowl and whisk them as you gradually pour in
about half of the pastry cream. Whisk the egg yolk mixture back into the saucepan
and place over low heat. Stirring constantly, cook a minute or two longer to thicken
a little more. Remove from the heat and stir in the butter and vanilla. Half submerge
the pan in a shallow bowl of cold water and stir to cool slightly.

3. Pour the freshly made pastry cream into the cooled pie shell and sift the confectioner's sugar over the top to prevent a skin from forming. Cool to room temperature and then chill until set.

4. Pick over the blueberries and then rinse and drain them. Place 2 pints of berries on paper towels to dry. Place the remaining pint of berries in a heavy medium-sized saucepan over moderate heat. Crush the berries with a potato masher or a fork and bring to a boil. Boil, stirring frequently, for about 2 minutes, until juicy. Place a sieve over a bowl and force the berries through. You should have 1 cup of syrupy juice; if you have more, reserve some for another use and if you have less, add water to make one cup.

5. On a sheet of waxed paper combine the granulated sugar and cornstarch, mixing them together with your fingers. Place the blueberry juice in a medium-sized saucepan. With a fork or a whisk, gradually blend in the sugar-cornstarch mixture until smooth. Add the orange zest and cook over moderate heat, stirring constantly, until boiling and thick. Boil for a minute or two, until translucent. Remove from the heat.

6. Reserve one cup of the two pints of whole berries for garnish. Arrange half of the remaining berries over the chilled pastry cream in the shell. Drizzle with half of the hot syrup. Arrange the other half of the berries over the glaze and drizzle with the remaining hot glaze. Scatter the reserved one cup of berries over the top. Chill until set, about 3 hours. Serve cold.

Aunt Irma's Raspberry Tart

This spectacular dessert makes the very best use of precious fresh raspberries when they are in season, and is suitable for the most formal occasion. Aunt Irma sometimes used small 3½-inch tart pans to make individual raspberry tarts for her guests.

MAKES ONE 9-INCH TART

SWEET PASTRY

1 cup all-purpose flour
2 tablespoons granulated sugar
Pinch of salt
8 tablespoons (1 stick) chilled
    unsalted butter, sliced

1 egg yolk
1 tablespoon water

PASTRY CREAM

¼ cup granulated sugar
3 tablespoons all-purpose flour
½ cup milk
½ cup heavy cream

4 egg yolks
4 tablespoons unsalted butter
2 teaspoons vanilla extract
1 teaspoon grated orange zest

FRUIT

3 cups fresh raspberries, picked over

½ cup raspberry jelly

1. Position a rack in the center of the oven and preheat to 425°F. To prepare the pastry, combine the flour, sugar, and a pinch of salt in a medium-sized bowl. With a pastry blender or two knives, cut in the butter until the mixture resembles coarse meal. In a cup, stir together the egg yolk with 1 tablespoon water; add to the flour mixture and stir with a fork to make a soft dough. Press evenly onto the bottom and up the sides of a 9-inch fluted tart pan with a removable bottom. If the dough is too soft to work with, simply chill briefly and continue. With a fork, prick the bottom all over. Bake until crisp and golden brown, 12 to 14 minutes. Cool on a rack.

2. Prepare the pastry cream: In a heavy medium-sized saucepan combine the sugar and flour. In a small bowl combine the milk and heavy cream. Whisk the milk mixture into the sugar-flour mixture until smooth. Stir over moderate heat until the mixture comes to a boil, then reduce the heat and simmer 2 to 3 minutes. In a medium bowl whisk the egg yolks and whisk in about half of the hot mixture. Return all to the saucepan and simmer about 2 minutes longer. Remove from the heat and stir in butter, vanilla, and orange zest. Turn into a bowl, cover with plastic wrap placed directly on the surface, and cool for 1 hour.

3. To assemble the tart: Spread the pastry cream in the shell. Starting around the edge, arrange the raspberries in concentric circles to completely cover the pastry cream. In a small saucepan melt the jelly over moderate heat. Simmer 2 to 3 minutes to reduce slightly, then brush over the berries. Chill about 2 hours, to set the pastry cream. Serve cold, cut into wedges.

BERRY CRUMBLE PIE

More often than not, my mother made this excellent pie
with fresh blueberries, more abundant than other berries and considerably less
expensive. It may also be made with raspberries, blackberries, or, if you can find
them, fat fresh boysenberries.

MAKES ONE 9-INCH PIE

4 cups blueberries, blackberries,
   raspberries, or boysenberries
   (or any combination to equal
   4 cups)
2 tablespoons quick-cooking
   tapioca

½ cup granulated sugar
1 teaspoon grated orange zest
   (optional)

TOPPING

½ cup granulated sugar
½ cup all-purpose flour
1 teaspoon ground cinnamon

4 tablespoons (½ stick) unsalted
   butter, chilled and sliced

1 tablespoon confectioner's sugar
Heavy cream, whipped (optional)

1 unbaked single-crust pie shell
   (page 90), chilled

1. Adjust a rack to the center of the oven and preheat to 450°F.

2. Meanwhile, in a large bowl, combine the berries, tapioca, sugar, and orange zest;
gently toss and let stand for 15 minutes.

3. Prepare the topping: In a medium-sized bowl, combine the sugar, flour, and
cinnamon; cut in the butter with a pastry blender until evenly crumbly.

4. Turn the berry mixture into the prepared pie shell. With your fingers, crumble
the topping all over the filling. Bake for 10 minutes, then reduce the oven temperature to 350°F and bake about 30 minutes longer, until the crust and topping are
golden brown. Place on a rack and cool to room temperature.

5. Before serving, sift the confectioner's sugar over the top and cut into slices. Serve
with whipped cream if desired.

MOM'S APPLE PIE

My mother always made the very best apple pie from
the simple recipe given here. However, I must caution you that
the results you get will depend on the flavor, juiciness, and texture of the apples
you use, and to some extent on the weather (it is difficult to keep a crust flaky
for very long during humid weather). My mother always used the freshest possible
green cooking apples like Granny Smiths or greenings; and she sometimes
added a splash of apple cider to them, instead of water,
if they seemed a little dry.

MAKES ONE 9-INCH PIE

2½ pounds (5 to 7) tart green
   cooking apples, such as Granny
   Smiths, greenings or Baldwins
1 cup granulated sugar
3 tablespoons all-purpose flour
1 teaspoon ground cinnamon
½ teaspoon freshly grated nutmeg
¼ teaspoon salt

1 tablespoon lemon juice
Water or apple cider (optional)
2 tablespoons unsalted butter, cut
   into bits

Pastry for a double-crust pie
   (page 89)

GLAZE (optional)

1 egg yolk
1 teaspoon water

1 tablespoon granulated sugar

1. Position a rack in the center of the oven and preheat to 425°F. On a lightly floured surface roll out one-half of the pastry to a 12-inch round. Fold in half or in quarters in order to transfer to a 9-inch pie pan. Unfold and ease the pastry into the pan without stretching it; there will be a generous overhang all around. Refrigerate until the oven is preheated and the apple filling is prepared.

2. Peel the apples and quarter them lengthwise. Core them and cut into wedges about ½-inch thick (you will have about 7 cups). In a large bowl combine the sugar, flour, cinnamon, nutmeg, and salt; add the apples and toss well. Add the lemon juice, and if the mixture seems dry, add about a tablespoon of water or apple cider. Turn the apple filling into the pastry-lined pie pan, mounding it in the center. Dot with butter.

3. On a lightly floured surface, roll out the remaining piece of pastry to a 12-inch round. Lightly moisten the edge of the bottom crust all around with cold water. Place the top pastry over the apples and press the two crusts together all around. Tightly roll the overhanging pastry under all around to make a raised edge. Flute decoratively with your fingertips or crimp with a fork. Cut three or four ¾-inch steam vents in the center with the tip of a paring knife.

4. In a small bowl stir together the egg yolk and water. Brush the top crust with the egg yolk glaze twice, and sprinkle with the sugar. Place pie on a baking sheet and bake for 20 minutes; reduce the oven temperature to 350°F and bake 20 to 30 minutes longer, until pie is golden brown and the apples are tender when pierced with a knife through a steam vent. Cool on a rack before serving. Serve with vanilla ice cream if desired.

Aunt Charlotte's Best Apricot Pie

The secret to the preparation of this pie
is the poaching of the apricots in pineapple juice, which lends the fruit an exquisite added flavor dimension. The pie also looks beautiful with its lattice top. In order to duplicate the flavor of this most wonderful pie, you must be sure to use fresh fruit at the height of the apricot season.

MAKES ONE 9-INCH PIE

1¼ cups unsweetened pineapple
  juice
¾ cup granulated sugar
2 pounds (16 to 20 small)
  unpeeled apricots, halved and
  pitted
2 tablespoons cornstarch
3 tablespoons cold water

3 tablespoons unsalted butter, cut
  into bits
2 teaspoons vanilla extract
¼ teaspoon salt

Pastry for a double-crust pie
  (page 89)

GLAZE (optional)

1 egg yolk
1 teaspoon water

1 tablespoon granulated sugar

1. In a heavy medium-sized saucepan (not aluminum or cast iron) combine the pineapple juice and sugar. Stirring over moderate heat, bring to a boil. Reduce the heat and simmer 1 minute. Working in batches to avoid crowding the pan, poach the apricot halves for about 3 minutes, just until tender. Place a strainer over a bowl. Remove the apricots with a slotted spoon as they are done and drain in the strainer. Measure the juices in the bowl and the pan; you should have 1 cup (if necessary, discard some to make a cup or add water or pineapple juice to make 1 cup).

2. In a small bowl stir the cornstarch with 3 tablespoons cold water until smooth. Place the 1 cup reserved juice in a small heavy saucepan and stir in the cornstarch mixture until smooth. Place over moderate heat and cook, stirring constantly, until juice comes to a boil and has thickened; boil for 1 minute. Remove from the heat and stir in the butter, vanilla, and salt, continuing to stir until butter melts. Turn into a large bowl and fold in the poached apricots. Cool to room temperature.

3. On a lightly floured surface, roll out the larger piece of pastry to a 12-inch round. Fold in half or quarters in order to transfer to a 9-inch pie pan. Unfold and ease the pastry into the pan without stretching it; there will be a generous overhang all around. Refrigerate until the oven is preheated.

4. Position a rack in the lower half of the oven and preheat to 450°F. On a lightly floured surface, roll out the remaining piece of pastry to an 11- or 12-inch round. Using either a pastry wheel with a zigzag edge or a sharp knife, cut the pastry into strips about ¾ inch wide; keep refrigerated until needed.

5. Turn the apricot filling into the pastry-lined pie pan. Evenly space 5 of the pastry strips in one direction over the filling, using the longest strips in the middle. Using 5 more strips, weave a lattice top over the pie. Attach the ends of the strips to the overhanging pastry by dipping your finger in water and moistening the overhang all around; press together. Tightly roll upward all around to make a raised edge and crimp or flute.

6. In a small bowl stir together the egg yolk and water. Brush the lattice (but not the fluted edge) with the egg yolk glaze twice and sprinkle lattice with the sugar. Place the pie on a baking sheet and bake for 10 minutes. Lower the oven temperature to 350°F and bake 25 to 30 minutes longer, until the crust is golden brown. Cool on a rack to room temperature or serve while just barely warm, with vanilla ice cream if desired.

PEACH PIE

Quite simply, this is the best peach pie I've ever eaten. Of course you must begin with beautiful tree-ripened fruit for the best results. We served it ever so slightly warm, with vanilla ice cream or perhaps with cold milk.

MAKES ONE 9-INCH PIE

6 to 8 large ripe freestone
  peaches (about 6 ounces each)
¾ cup granulated sugar
2 tablespoons all-purpose flour
2 tablespoons cornstarch
½ teaspoon ground cinnamon
½ teaspoon grated nutmeg

¼ teaspoon salt
1 tablespoon fresh lemon juice
2 tablespoons unsalted butter, cut
  into bits

Pastry for a double-crust pie
  (page 89)

GLAZE (optional)

1 egg yolk

1 teaspoon water

1. Adjust a rack one-third up from the bottom of the oven and preheat to 425°F Line a baking sheet with aluminum foil.

2. Bring a medium-sized pot of water to a boil over high heat; add two or three peaches and blanch for 10 to 30 seconds (depending on the ripeness), then rinse under cold water. Repeat with remaining peaches. Peel and cut into slices about ½-inch thick or slightly thicker; you will need about 5 cups.

3. On a lightly floured surface, roll out the larger portion of dough into a round about 12 inches in diameter. Loosely drape it into a 9-inch pie pan (4- to 4½-cup capacity) and, without stretching the dough, fit it to conform to the pie pan; there should be a generous overhang all around. Refrigerate until needed. Roll out the remaining piece of pastry to an 11- to 12-inch round. With a pastry wheel or a knife, cut into strips about ¾ inch wide. Refrigerate until needed.

4. In a large bowl combine the sugar, flour, cornstarch, cinnamon, nutmeg, and salt; stir together until blended. Add the peaches, lemon juice, and butter bits and toss gently but thoroughly. Turn into the lined pie pan.

5. Evenly space 5 strips of the pastry over the filling. Weave 5 more strips through, crosswise, to make a lattice top. Using a finger dipped in water, moisten the underside of the ends of the pastry strips and press them to the overhanging pastry all around. Tightly roll up all around to make a raised edge and then flute or crimp.

6. If glazing the pie crust, beat the egg yolk in a small bowl with 1 teaspoon of water and paint onto the lattice strips but not the fluted edge. One yolk will be enough to glaze three pies. Place on a baking sheet and bake 25 to 30 minutes, until light golden brown. Reduce the heat to 350°F and bake about 20 minutes longer, until golden brown and bubbly. Cool on a rack.

BLACKBERRY PIE

Blackberries can be precious, there's no question about it.
They can also be plentiful if you have a blackberry bramble. This pie was a treat we had only once a year, at the height of blackberry season. The berries are thickened the old-fashioned way, with flour.

MAKES ONE 9-INCH PIE

5 cups fresh blackberries
Scant cup granulated sugar
3 tablespoons all-purpose flour
1 tablespoon cornstarch
½ teaspoon ground cinnamon

½ teaspoon salt
⅛ teaspoon almond extract
2 tablespoons butter, cut into bits

Pastry for a double-crust pie (page 89)

GLAZE (optional)

1 egg yolk   1 teaspoon water

1. Adjust a rack one-third up from the bottom of the oven and preheat to 425°F.

2. Pick over the blackberries, and if they are dirty, quickly rinse and drain on paper towels.

3. On a lightly floured surface, roll out the larger portion of dough into a round about 12 inches in diameter. Loosely drape it into a 9-inch pie pan (4- to 4½-cup capacity) and, without stretching the dough, fit it to conform to the pie pan; there should be a generous overhang all around. Refrigerate until needed. On a lightly floured surface, roll out the remaining piece of pastry to an 11- to 12-inch round.

With a pastry wheel or a knife, cut the pastry into strips about ¾ inch wide. Refrigerate until needed.

4. To make a "scant" cup of sugar, remove about 2 tablespoons from a level cup of sugar. In a large bowl, combine the sugar, flour, cornstarch, cinnamon, and salt. Add the berries and the almond extract and gently toss together. Add the butter bits and toss once more. Turn into the pastry-lined pie pan.

5. Evenly space 5 strips of pastry over the filling. Weave 5 more strips through, crosswise, to make a lattice top. Using a finger dipped in water, moisten the underside of the ends of the pastry strips and press them to the overhanging pastry all around. Tightly roll up all around to make a raised edge and then flute or crimp.

6. If glazing the pie crust, beat the egg yolk in a small bowl with 1 teaspoon of water and paint onto the lattice strips but not the fluted edge (one yolk is enough to glaze three pies). Place on a baking sheet and bake 20 to 25 minutes, until light golden brown. Reduce the heat to 350°F and bake 20 to 25 minutes longer, until golden brown and bubbly. Cool on a rack.

RHUBARB PIE

The distinctive sweet and tangy aroma of rhubarb cooking in my cousin Leta Jo's kitchen was always a sure sign that spring had officially arrived. Not only does this pie slice excellently, it sports a beautiful glazed lattice top as well.

MAKES ONE 9-INCH PIE

1¼ pounds fresh rhubarb, cut in
  ¾-inch pieces to make 4 cups
1⅓ cups granulated sugar
¼ cup all-purpose flour
1½ teaspoons grated orange zest
  (see Note)
½ teaspoon grated nutmeg

¼ teaspoon ground cinnamon
¼ teaspoon salt
3 large eggs, slightly beaten
2 tablespoons butter, cut into bits

Pastry for a double-crust pie
  (page 89)

GLAZE (optional)

1 egg yolk   1 teaspoon water

1. Adjust an oven rack to the center of the oven; preheat to 425°F.

2. On a lightly floured surface, roll out the larger portion of dough into a round 12 to 13 inches in diameter. Loosely drape it into a 9-inch pie pan (4- to 4½-cup capacity) and, without stretching the dough, lightly press it to conform to the pan; there will be a generous overhang all around. Refrigerate until needed. On a lightly floured surface, roll out the remaining piece of pastry to an 11- to 12-inch round. With a pastry wheel or a knife, cut the pastry into strips about ¾ inch wide. Refrigerate until needed.

3. In a large bowl, combine the rhubarb, sugar, flour, orange zest, nutmeg, cinnamon, and salt; stir in the eggs to blend and fold in the butter.

4. Turn the rhubarb filling into the prepared pie shell. Evenly space 5 strips of pastry over the filling and weave 5 more through them to make a lattice top. Working around the edge, moisten the undersides of the ends of the strips and press them to the overhanging pastry; tightly roll up all around and decoratively crimp to seal.

5. If glazing the pie crust, beat the egg yolk in a small bowl with 1 teaspoon of water and paint onto the lattice strips but not the fluted edge (one egg yolk is enough to glaze three pies). Bake for 10 to 15 minutes, until light golden brown. Reduce the oven temperature to 350°F and bake 30 to 40 minutes longer, until golden brown and bubbly. Transfer to a rack and cool for 1 hour or longer. Serve warm or at room temperature.

Note: Zest, the orange outer layer of orange peel, is easiest to remove with a zester, a tool that has 5 tiny holes designed for scraping the peel. Finely chop the strands of zest with a knife. If you don't have this tool, simply grate the rind.

Grandma's Sour Cherry Pie

Sour cherries are regaining popularity these days, making it easier to find them in many localities than it has been for some time. Their season is short, so take advantage when you can by preparing this wonderful pie.

MAKES ONE 9-INCH PIE

2 pounds (6 cups) fresh sour
cherries
½ cup to ¾ cup granulated sugar
2 tablespoons all-purpose flour
1 tablespoon cornstarch
Pinch of ground cinnamon

2 tablespoons chilled unsalted
butter, cut into bits

Pastry for a double-crust pie
(page 89)

GLAZE (optional)

1 egg yolk   1 teaspoon water

1. Rinse the cherries and pull out the stems. Using a cherry pitter or a hairpin, pit the cherries into a colander or strainer. Place over a bowl and let cherries drain for about 15 minutes, discarding any juice (or reserving it for another use). You will have about 4 cups of pitted cherries.

2. Adjust a rack to the center of the oven and preheat to 425°F.

3. On a lightly floured surface, roll out the larger portion of dough into a round that measures about 12 inches in diameter. Loosely drape it into a 9-inch pie pan (4- to 4½-cup capacity) and, without stretching the dough, press it lightly to conform to the pan; there should be a generous overhang all around. Refrigerate until needed. Roll out the remaining piece of pastry into an 11- to 12-inch round; with a pastry wheel or knife, cut the pastry into strips about ¾ inch wide. Refrigerate until needed.

4. In a large bowl combine the drained pitted cherries with ½ cup of sugar, flour, cornstarch, and cinnamon; taste and add more sugar if desired. Toss to moisten and fold in the butter bits. Turn into the pastry-lined pie pan. Evenly space 5 strips of pastry in one direction over the filling. Using 5 more strips, weave a lattice top over the pie. Attach the ends of the strips to the overhanging pastry edge all around by dipping a finger into water and moistening the dough before pressing together. Tightly roll up all around and then crimp decoratively to seal.

5. If glazing the pie crust, beat the egg yolk with 1 teaspoon cold water and paint onto the lattice (but not the fluting) with a pastry brush (the glaze will be enough to glaze three pies). Place on a baking sheet and bake for 20 to 25 minutes, until pie begins to brown and become bubbly; reduce the heat to 350°F and bake until golden brown and done, 20 to 25 minutes longer. Transfer to a rack and cool to room temperature.

LEMON MERINGUE PIE

This is not a recipe from the family archives, but one that I developed over the course of many years. It has proved to be a great favorite, and since I've never found a better recipe for lemon meringue pie, I am including it here.

MAKES ONE 9-INCH PIE

1 cup granulated sugar
5 tablespoons cornstarch
¼ teaspoon salt
4 egg yolks (set aside whites for meringue)
½ cup fresh lemon juice

2 cups cold water
1½ teaspoons grated lemon zest
5 tablespoons unsalted butter, sliced

1 single-crust pie shell (page 90), baked and cooled

MERINGUE

4 egg whites
¼ teaspoon cream of tartar

¼ teaspoon salt
½ cup granulated sugar

1. In a heavy medium-sized saucepan stir together the sugar, cornstarch, salt, egg yolks, and lemon juice. Add 2 cups of cold water and whisk until well blended. Cook over moderate heat, whisking or stirring constantly, until the mixture comes to a full boil. Cook, stirring, for 1 minute. Remove from the heat and stir in the lemon zest and butter, stirring until butter melts. Pour the filling into the pie shell, place a round of waxed paper directly on the surface, and cool on a rack to room temperature.

2. Preheat the oven to 350°F. To make the meringue, combine the egg whites, cream of tartar and salt in a large bowl. Beat with an electric mixer until soft peaks begin to form. Gradually beat in the sugar and continue to beat until stiff glossy peaks form. Do not overbeat or the meringue will be dry.

3. Remove the waxed paper from the top of the pie filling. Pile the meringue over the filling and spread it to slightly overlap the fluted edge of the pie crust (this is important or meringue will shrink inward over the filling). Make decorative swirls with the back of a spoon. Bake until the top is pale golden brown, 12 to 15 minutes. Place on a rack and cool to room temperature. Refrigerate until just chilled and set, about 2 hours. Slice with a sharp knife dipped into hot water.

PUMPKIN PIE

My mother always used fresh pumpkin to make this
traditional pie. However, today's pumpkins make better jack o'lanterns
than pies—even those designated pie pumpkins are often tasteless. Nothing beats
a really good pumpkin for flavor, if you can find one; but if you don't want to take
a chance, use a butternut squash instead. Although the results won't be
quite as tasty, you can substitute canned pumpkin purée, cup for cup.

MAKES ONE 9-INCH PIE

One 3- to 4-pound pumpkin or a
  2½- to 3-pound butternut squash
¾ to 1 cup packed dark brown
  sugar
3 large eggs
1½ cups heavy cream

1½ teaspoons ground cinnamon
½ teaspoon freshly grated nutmeg
¼ teaspoon ground cloves
¼ teaspoon salt

Pastry for a single-crust pie shell (page 90)

1. Position a rack in the center of the oven and preheat to 400°F.

2. With a large heavy knife, cut the pumpkin or squash in half lengthwise. If using a pumpkin, cut the pieces in half again. Scoop out the seeds and fibers with a spoon. Add ¼ inch water to a 13-by-9-inch baking dish and arrange the pieces, cut side down, in it. Bake until very tender when pierced with a fork, about 45 minutes for the pumpkin or 1 hour for the butternut squash.

3. When cool enough to handle, or at room temperature, use a paring knife to peel off the skin. Purée in a food processor or put through a food mill or strainer. You will need 2 cups of purée for this pie.

4. While pumpkin is cooling, move the rack to the lower third of the oven and increase heat to 450°F.

5. On a lightly floured surface, roll the pastry into a thin round about 12 inches in diameter. Loosely drape it into a 9-inch pie pan and, without stretching it, fit the dough to the pan. Tightly roll the overhang under all around to make a high edge and crimp decoratively with your fingers. Line with a sheet of aluminum foil and fill with pie weights or dried beans or rice. Place on a baking sheet and bake for 8 to 10 minutes, until the edge has set. Remove the foil and weights and prick the bottom with a fork. Bake 5 minutes longer, until the bottom has set. Remove from the oven and reduce the temperature to 425°F.

6. In a large bowl beat together 2 cups pumpkin purée and ¾ cup of the sugar until blended. Whisk or beat in the eggs, heavy cream, cinnamon, nutmeg, cloves, and salt. Taste for sweetness and add up to ¼ cup more sugar if desired. Place the partially baked pie shell on a baking sheet and fill to the fluted edge with the pumpkin pie filling. Carefully place in the oven and bake 10 minutes. Reduce the heat to 300°F and bake until set, 35 to 45 minutes longer. Transfer to a rack and cool to room temperature. Cut into wedges and serve with whipped cream if desired.

PECAN PIE

This is a bit less sweet than most versions of pecan pie
because it contains one more egg than does the usual recipe. But it still qualifies
as sweet enough to fulfill the craving of any certified pecan-pie lover. Just be sure
to use the freshest pecans you can find.

MAKES ONE 9-INCH PIE

8 tablespoons (1 stick) unsalted
    butter
1 cup light corn syrup
¾ cup packed dark brown sugar
4 large eggs
1 tablespoon vanilla extract
¼ teaspoon salt

1 cup (4 ounces) chopped pecans
1 cup (4 ounces) pecan halves
Heavy cream (optional)

1 unbaked single-crust pie shell
(page 90)

1. After lining the pie pan with pastry, trim the rim so that there is only a ½-inch overhang all around, and tuck it under. Using the tines of a fork and working from the outside with the tines pointing inward, press the edge all around. Chill shell until needed.

2. In a small heavy saucepan combine the butter, corn syrup, and brown sugar. Place over low heat and, stirring constantly, cook until the sugar has dissolved. Remove from the heat and cool to room temperature.

3. Position a rack in the center of the oven and preheat to 325°F. In a large bowl whisk the eggs, vanilla, and salt together. Whisking constantly, pour in the cooled syrup in a steady stream until smooth.

4. Place the chopped pecans in the prepared shell and pour in the filling. Starting around the outside top edge, arrange the pecan halves in concentric circles, placing them directly on the filling. Set pie pan on a baking sheet and bake for about 1 hour, until the pie is puffed in the center and the edges are light golden brown. As the pie cools on a rack, it will level. Serve at room temperature, garnished with softly whipped unsweetened cream if desired.

Note: Fresh pecans purchased from a reliable purveyor make the best pies. Extra pecans stored in airtight containers in the freezer remain fresher than those sold in cans, bagged, or "loose."

MRS. PAASENEN'S CHEESE PIE

Here is the cheese pie that Farmer Paasenen's wife contributed
to summer picnics near his farm. Of course the legendary Paasenen pie
was made with homemade cheese and buttermilk, but this version, made with
milk and cheese from the supermarket, is quite delicious.

MAKES ONE 9-INCH PIE

One 3-ounce package cream cheese, softened to room temperature
⅔ cup granulated sugar
3 tablespoons all-purpose flour
3 tablespoons butter, melted
3 large eggs
1 cup buttermilk

1 cup half-and-half (or half milk, half cream)
¼ teaspoon salt
2 teaspoons vanilla extract

1 unbaked single-crust pie shell (page 90)

1. Position a rack in the center of the oven and preheat to 425°F. Line the pie shell with aluminum foil and fill with pie weights or dried beans or raw rice. Bake for 8 to 10 minutes, until the edge has set. Remove the foil and weights and continue baking, tapping pastry with a wooden spoon if it should bubble, for about 5 minutes longer, just until light golden brown. Remove the shell to a rack and decrease the oven temperature to 300°F.

2. In a large bowl, beat the cream cheese with an electric mixer until smooth. Add the sugar and flour and beat until smooth; beat in the melted butter. Beat in the eggs one at a time, then the buttermilk, half and half, salt, and vanilla. Turn into the hot shell, place on a baking sheet, and bake 55 to 60 minutes, until the center is just set. Cool on a rack to room temperature. Serve at room temperature or chilled.

CHOCOLATE CREAM PIE

Cream pies were always a hit in our house and this chocolate cream pie was at the top of the list. It has a deep rich chocolate flavor that is complemented by mounds of sweetened cream.

MAKES ONE 9-INCH PIE

3 cups milk
1 cup granulated sugar
2 tablespoons all-purpose flour
2 tablespoons cornstarch
1/4 teaspoon salt
3 egg yolks
3 tablespoons unsalted butter, sliced

2 teaspoons vanilla extract
4 ounces (4 squares) unsweetened chocolate, chopped

1 Cookie Crumb Shell (page 91), baked and cooled or 1 single-crust pie shell (page 90), baked and cooled

TOPPING

1 1/2 cups heavy cream
1/4 to 1/2 cup sifted confectioner's sugar

1/2 teaspoon vanilla extract
Chocolate shavings (optional), see Note

1. In a heavy medium-sized saucepan scald the milk over moderately low heat just until very small bubbles show around the edges of the milk's surface.

2. In a heavy medium-sized saucepan stir together the sugar, flour, cornstarch, and salt; whisking constantly, pour in the hot milk in a steady stream. Cook over moderate heat, stirring constantly, until very thick; bring to a boil. Remove from the heat. In a medium-sized bowl whisk the egg yolks and gradually whisk in about 2 cups of the hot mixture; return to the saucepan and, stirring constantly, simmer for 2 to 3 minutes, until slightly thicker. Remove from the heat and stir in the butter, vanilla, and chocolate, continuing to stir until the butter and chocolate have melted.

Pour into a bowl, cover with plastic wrap or waxed paper placed directly on the surface, and cool for about 30 minutes. Stir the filling and pour into the shell; cover again and cool to room temperature. Chill thoroughly, at least 2 hours.

3. Prepare the topping: Place a deep medium-sized bowl and beaters in the freezer for about 15 minutes. Beat the cream just until soft peaks form and then add ¼ cup of the sugar and beat in just until blended. Taste for sweetness and add up to ¼ cup more sugar if desired (it can be a little on the sweet side to compensate for the bittersweet chocolate filling). Beat in the vanilla, beating just until stiff. Cover the pie with the whipped cream, making rosettes around the edge, if desired, using a pastry bag fitted with a star tip. Garnish with chocolate shavings if you wish, and serve cold.

Note: A block of chocolate can be softened just enough for shaving by placing it about a foot from the heat of a lighted bulb. You can make chocolate curls by drawing a knife, metal pastry scraper, or swivel-bladed vegetable peeler across the block's surface. Chill the curls on a small plate before handling.

AUNT MYRA'S BUTTERSCOTCH PIE

An incredibly rich pie filling is lightened by mounds of meringue in this very old and much favored family recipe.

MAKES ONE 9-INCH PIE

1 cup packed light brown sugar
⅓ cup all-purpose flour
¼ teaspoon salt
One 12- to 13-ounce can
   evaporated milk
Water
4 egg yolks (reserve whites for
   meringue)

4 tablespoons (½ stick) unsalted
   butter, cut in pieces
1 teaspoon vanilla

1 single-crust pie shell (page 90),
   baked and cooled

MERINGUE

4 egg whites, at room temperature
¼ teaspoon salt

¼ teaspoon cream of tartar
½ cup granulated sugar

1. Place the brown sugar, flour, and salt in a large bowl. Add enough water to the evaporated milk to measure 2 cups. In a small bowl, beat the egg yolks and then whisk in ½ cup of the diluted milk. Whisk the egg-milk mixture into the dry ingredients until thoroughly blended and then whisk in the remaining milk. Transfer to the top of a double boiler over simmering water. Whisk or stir constantly until very thick, 10 to 15 minutes. Remove from the heat and stir in the butter and vanilla, continuing to stir until the butter melts. Place a round of waxed paper directly on the surface and cool for 15 minutes. Pour into the baked pie shell and cover with a round of waxed paper. Let cool to room temperature and then refrigerate until well chilled, about 3 hours.

2. Prepare the meringue: Preheat the oven to 350°F. In a large bowl, beat the egg whites with the salt and cream of tartar until soft peaks form. Gradually add the sugar and continue beating until the whites are stiff and glossy. Do not overbeat or the meringue will be dry and lumpy.

3. Remove the waxed paper from the pie filling and pile the meringue on top, mounding it in the center, swirling decoratively, and spreading it out to overlap the crust slightly all around to discourage shrinking.

4. Bake the pie in the center of the oven until golden, about 12 to 15 minutes. Cool on a rack and then refrigerate for 2 to 3 hours before serving. When slicing, dip a sharp knife in very hot water before making each cut.

COCONUT CREAM PIE

If you have never tasted a coconut cream pie
made with fresh coconut, by all means try this one. It takes a long time to make,
but the result is superb. Packaged coconut, which is preshredded and presweetened,
really isn't an adequate substitute for fresh in this pie.

MAKES ONE 9-INCH PIE

1 fresh medium-sized coconut
2½ cups milk
¾ cup granulated sugar
3 tablespoons all-purpose flour
2 tablespoons cornstarch

4 egg yolks (set aside whites for meringue)
3 tablespoons unsalted butter
2 teaspoons vanilla extract

1 single-crust pie shell (page 90),
  baked and cooled

MERINGUE

4 egg whites
¼ teaspoon cream of tartar

¼ teaspoon salt
½ cup granulated sugar

1. Position a rack in the lower third of the oven and preheat to 375°F. Using a hammer and nail, puncture the three eyes of the coconut and drain, upside down, over a cup. Discard the liquid (or reserve for another use). Bake the coconut for 10 minutes. Wrap it in a towel and, with a hammer, crack it to separate the flesh from the shell, prying out the pieces with a paring knife. Rinse the pieces and peel with a swivel-bladed vegetable peeler. Rinse again, then shred through the coarse side of a cheese grater. You will have about 4 cups.

2. Measure the shredded coconut and divide it, setting aside 1½ cups to make toasted coconut and placing the remaining 2½ cups in a heatproof bowl. In a heavy medium-sized saucepan over moderate heat, scald the milk until small bubbles show around the edges of the surface. Pour milk over the coconut and let stand 5 minutes to soften. Rinse a triple layer of cheesecloth under cold water and wring out. Line a sieve with the cheesecloth and place it over a bowl. Purée half of the coconut-milk mixture in a blender, and pour through the lined sieve. Purée the remaining coconut-milk mixture and pour through the sieve. Gather up the cheesecloth to enclose the coconut and squeeze out as much liquid as possible, wringing it out tightly. Discard the solids in the cheesecloth. You should have 3 cups of coconut cream; if you do not, add milk to make 3 cups.

3. Preheat the oven to 350°F. Arrange the reserved 1½ cups shredded coconut on a baking sheet and toast, stirring once in a while, until light golden brown, 12 to 15 minutes. Cool.

4. In a heavy medium-sized saucepan stir together the sugar, flour, and cornstarch. In a steady stream, whisk in the 3 cups coconut cream until smooth. Place over moderate heat and cook, stirring constantly, until the mixture thickens and begins to simmer. Place the egg yolks in a medium bowl and whisk them. Gradually whisk in about half of the cooked coconut mixture and return to the pan. Cook, stirring, until the mixture comes to a boil and then simmer 2 to 3 minutes, until thickened further. Remove from the heat and stir in the butter and vanilla, continuing to stir until the butter melts. Reserve ¼ cup of the toasted coconut for the top of the meringue and stir the remainder into the filling. Turn into a shallow bowl, cover with a sheet of waxed paper or plastic wrap placed directly on the surface, and cool for 30 minutes. Turn into the prepared shell, cover with waxed paper or plastic wrap, and cool to room temperature. Chill 4 hours or overnight. Peel off the paper.

5. Prepare the meringue: Position a rack in the lower half of the oven and preheat to 350°F. Place the egg whites in a large deep bowl along with the cream of tartar and salt. With an electric mixer beat until soft peaks begin to form. Gradually beat in the sugar and continue beating until stiff glossy peaks form; do not overbeat or the meringue will be lumpy and dry. Spoon over the pie, overlapping the crust all around so it will not shrink inward and mounding it slightly in the middle. Make decorative swirls with the back of a spoon. Scatter the reserved ¼ cup toasted coconut shreds over the top. Bake about 12 minutes, or until golden brown. Cool on a rack and then chill just until cold, about 2 hours. To slice, dip a knife in very hot water to mark slices, redipping knife between each cut; after the slices have been marked, cut through the filling and crust and remove the wedges with a pie server.

Note: Coconut cream pies are traditionally topped with whipped cream; you can easily substitute whipped cream for the meringue topping by following instructions on page 82 of the chocolate cream pie recipe.

BANANA MERINGUE PIE

This banana cream pie with its meringue topping has always been my father's favorite. If you prefer, top the chilled filling with whipped cream instead of meringue.

MAKES ONE 9-INCH PIE

¾ cup granulated sugar
6 tablespoons all-purpose flour
¼ teaspoon salt
2 cups milk, scalded
4 egg yolks (set aside whites for meringue)
4 tablespoons (½ stick) unsalted butter, sliced

1 teaspoon vanilla extract
3 large or 4 small bananas, sliced ¼ inch thick

1 single-crust pie shell, flaky or cookie crumb, (pages 90, 91), baked and cooled

MERINGUE

4 large egg whites
¼ teaspoon salt

¼ teaspoon cream of tartar
½ cup sugar

1. Prepare the filling: In a heavy medium-sized saucepan, combine the sugar, flour, and salt. Gradually whisk in the hot milk until smooth. Stirring constantly over moderate heat, bring the mixture to a boil. Cook for 1 minute, stirring constantly, and then remove from the heat. Place the egg yolks in a medium-sized bowl and whisk them as you slowly pour in about 1 cup of the hot mixture. Whisk the mixture back into the saucepan and place over low heat. Cook, stirring constantly, to thicken a little more, 2 to 3 minutes longer. Remove from the heat and stir in the butter and vanilla, continuing to stir until butter melts. To prevent a skin from forming, place a round of waxed paper directly on the surface; allow to cool at room temperature for 20 to 30 minutes.

2. Arrange half of the banana slices, overlapping slightly, over the bottom of the pie shell. Cover them evenly with half of the cream filling, and top with the remaining banana slices. Cover with the remaining cream filling. Place waxed paper on top and cool to room temperature; then refrigerate for 2 hours.

3. Adjust a rack to the lower third of the oven and preheat to 350°F.

4. Prepare the meringue: In a large mixing bowl, combine the egg whites, salt, and cream of tartar. With an electric mixer, beat until soft peaks form. Gradually add the sugar and continue beating until stiff glossy peaks form; do not overbeat or the meringue will be dry.

5. Remove the waxed paper from the pie. Spoon the meringue over the filling, mounding it a bit in the center and spreading to slightly overlap the edge of the pie shell all around (this is important or it will shrink inward over the filling). Make decorative swirls with the back of a spoon, and bake until the top is pale golden brown, 12 to 15 minutes. Place on a rack and cool to room temperature. Refrigerate until chilled and set, 2 to 3 hours. To slice, dip a sharp knife into very hot tap water and cut through the meringue to mark the slices, redipping the knife in hot water between each cut; after the slices have been marked, use the same knife to cut through the filling and crust. Serve cold.

RASPBERRY CREAM PIE

Aromatic, cool, and refreshing, this pie
has a rich flavor and deep color. Raspberries and cream, flavored with vanilla,
is to my mind a marriage made in heaven.

MAKES ONE 9-INCH PIE

One ¼-ounce envelope unflavored
  gelatin
½ cup cold water
3 cups (1½ pints) fresh
  raspberries
¾ cup granulated sugar
2 tablespoons cornstarch

1 cup heavy cream
1 tablespoon lemon juice
1 teaspoon vanilla extract

1 Cookie Crumb Shell (page 91),
  baked and cooled

TOPPING

1½ cups heavy cream
¼ cup sifted confectioner's sugar

8 raspberries, for garnish

1. In a small cup sprinkle the gelatin over ¼ cup cold water; let soften.

2. In a heavy medium-sized saucepan combine 2 cups of the raspberries with ¼ cup of water. Bring to a boil over moderately high heat, stirring and mashing, and boil for 2 minutes. Place a sieve over a bowl and force the berries through. Scrape the pulp from the underside of the sieve into the bowl; discard the seeds. You should have 1 cup of juicy raspberry purée; if you have less, add water to make 1 cup.

3. On a sheet of waxed paper, combine the sugar and cornstarch, mixing them together with your fingers. Place the raspberry purée and heavy cream in a small heavy saucepan and gradually whisk in the sugar-cornstarch until smooth. Place over moderate heat and cook, stirring constantly, until the mixture boils and becomes thick and translucent; boil 1 minute longer. Remove from the heat and stir in the lemon juice, vanilla, and softened gelatin until smooth. Transfer to a medium bowl and chill, stirring frequently, until beginning to set (the mixture will resemble unbeaten egg whites in consistency). Stir in the remaining 1 cup raspberries and pour the filling into the pie shell. Chill thoroughly, until set, at least 3 hours or as long as overnight.

4. Prepare the topping: Using a chilled bowl and beaters, whip the 1½ cups cream until soft peaks form. Gradually add the confectioner's sugar and beat until just stiff. If desired, reserve about 1 cup of the whipped cream for piping. With a spatula, spread the rest evenly over the filling. Using a pastry bag with a ¼-inch star tip, or a spoon, pipe or spoon 7 mounds of whipped cream around the edge of the pie and one large mound in the center. Garnish each mound with a raspberry. Serve cold.

LEMON CHIFFON PIE

The whipped cream in this chiffon pie
adds richness and flavor. I can still recall how my mother folded in a quantity
of whipped cream just before turning the filling into a cookie crumb pie shell.
More whipped cream is spooned in dollops around the top
and the whole is garnished with lemon slices.

MAKES ONE 9-INCH PIE

¼ cup cold water
One ¼-ounce envelope unflavored
   gelatin
4 large eggs, separated
¾ cup granulated sugar
1 teaspoon grated lemon zest

½ cup fresh lemon juice
¼ teaspoon salt
½ cup heavy cream

Cookie Crumb Shell (page 91),
   baked and cooled

TOPPING

½ cup heavy cream
3 tablespoons confectioner's sugar

½ teaspoon vanilla extract
4 thin lemon slices, halved, for garnish

1. Place ¼ cup of cold water in a small bowl or a cup and sprinkle the gelatin over it; stir to moisten and let it soften until needed.

2. In the top of a double boiler, off the heat, whisk the egg yolks with ½ cup of the sugar; whisk in the lemon zest and lemon juice. Place over simmering water and stir constantly until thickened, about 10 minutes. Remove from the heat and stir in the softened gelatin until melted and smooth. Turn into a bowl and, stirring often, cool just until syrupy; this can be done over a bowl of ice or in the refrigerator (if it should happen to set, however, you will have to melt it over simmering water and then rechill to the syrupy stage).

3. Meanwhile, place the egg whites and salt in a large deep mixing bowl. Beat with an electric mixer until soft peaks just begin to form. Gradually beat in the remaining ¼ cup sugar and beat until stiff glossy peaks form. In a small deep bowl, beat the ½ cup cream just until stiff. Fold about one-fourth of the egg whites into the syrupy mixture. Then fold the mixture into the remaining whites. Quickly fold in the whipped cream. Turn into the prepared shell and chill until set. (If possible, place in the freezer for 5 to 10 minutes to help the gelatin set and then place in the refrigerator.)

4. Prepare the topping: Using chilled bowl and beaters, whip the cream until almost stiff. Add the confectioner's sugar and beat just until stiff, then stir in the vanilla. Using a spoon or a pastry bag fitted with a ½-inch star tip, spoon or pipe the whipped cream in seven mounds around the top and one in the center. Push one half-slice of lemon into each mound and serve cold.

FLAKY PASTRY

This flaky pastry crust is easy to make and work with; for an interesting flavor, you may want to substitute about two tablespoons of lard for the same amount of butter.

ENOUGH FOR A 9-INCH DOUBLE-CRUST PIE

2¼ cups all-purpose flour
½ teaspoon salt
¾ cup vegetable shortening or 6
    tablespoons each of shortening
    and chilled sliced butter

5 to 6 tablespoons ice water

1. In a large bowl combine the flour and salt. Using a pastry blender or two knives, cut in the shortening until the mixture resembles coarse meal. Sprinkle with 3 tablespoons of the ice water and stir quickly with a fork, just to moisten. Sprinkle on another 2 tablespoons water and quickly stir in. Add just enough of the remaining water to make a dough that holds together. Divide in two, making one piece slightly larger than the other. Wrap in waxed paper or plastic wrap and chill for an hour or as long as a day or two.

FLAKY PASTRY

ENOUGH FOR A 9-INCH SINGLE-CRUST PIE

1½ cups all-purpose flour
¼ teaspoon salt
½ cup vegetable shortening or
 ¼ cup shortening and ¼ cup
 chilled unsalted butter, sliced

3 to 4 tablespoons ice water

1. In a large bowl stir together the flour and salt. Using a pastry blender or two knives, cut in the shortening until the mixture resembles coarse meal. Sprinkle with 2 tablespoons of the ice water (toss ice cubes with water to make sure it's good and icy) and stir quickly with a fork, just to moisten. Sprinkle another tablespoon of water over the top and quickly stir in. Add just enough of the remaining water to make a dough that holds together. On a sheet of waxed paper, flatten into a 6-inch disk, cover, and chill for about 1 hour or as long as a day or two.

ROLLING AND BAKING A SINGLE-CRUST PIE SHELL

1. Adjust a rack to the center of the oven and preheat to 425°F.

2. On a lightly floured surface, roll out the pastry for a single 9-inch pie shell to a thin round about 12 inches in diameter. Loosely drape into a 9-inch pie pan and ease in without stretching the dough. Roll the underhanging pastry tightly under all around and crimp to make a decorative edge.

3. For a baked shell, line with aluminum foil and fill with pie weights or dried beans or rice. Place on a baking sheet and bake for 10 to 12 minutes, until the edge has set. Remove the foil and weights and return the shell to the oven for about 5 minutes, until the bottom is firm and light golden brown. Tap the bottom with a wooden spoon if it should bubble up. Cool on a rack to room temperature.

Note: If the pastry should tear or break, it is easily patchable; simply moisten the area surrounding the tear with water and press another piece on top. When it is baked, the pastry will appear flawless.

In general, handle the pastry as little as possible; do not reroll or the pastry will be tough.

LATTICE-TOPPED PIES

1. On a lightly floured surface, roll the pastry to an 11- or 12-inch round. With a knife or a pastry wheel with a crimped edge, cut the pastry into strips about ¾-inch wide, using a ruler; keep refrigerated until needed.

2. Fill the pastry-lined pie pan with the appropriate filling. Evenly space 5 strips of pastry in one direction over the filling, using the longest strips in the middle. Using 5 more strips, weave a lattice top over the pie as follows: Of the 5 pastry strips already on the pie, fold strips 1, 3, and 5 (every other one) in half back over themselves. Lay the longest of the five remaining strips perpendicularly across the center of the pie. Unfold the 3 folded strips and then fold in half back over themselves the 2 that were not folded. Add another horizontal strip and unfold the two folded strips. In this manner, a lattice weave is created, working from the center outward. After you have woven in 5 strips in each direction, attach the ends to the overhanging pastry by dipping your finger in water and moistening the overhang all around; press together. Tightly roll up all around to make a raised edge and crimp or flute.

Cookie crumb shell

MAKES ONE 9-INCH SHELL

1⅓ cups finely crushed vanilla
    cookie crumbs, such as vanilla
    wafers
2 tablespoons granulated sugar

½ teaspoon vanilla extract
5 tablespoons unsalted butter,
    melted

1. Adjust a rack to the center of the oven and preheat to 350°F. Butter the inside bottom of a 9-inch pie pan (do not butter the sides or the shell will slump).

2. In a medium-sized bowl combine the cookie crumbs, sugar, and vanilla. Add the butter and toss until the crumbs are evenly coated.

3. Turn the mixture into the prepared pie pan. Scatter the crumbs so that they are evenly distributed and press onto bottom and up sides to make an even shell. Bake for 8 minutes, until set and just barely beginning to brown. Cool to room temperature on a rack.

QUICK BREADS
❧ AND COFFEE CAKES ❧

Quick breads include a wonderful array of coffee cakes, muffins, and biscuits that—true to their billing—are quickly and easily prepared. Most can be put together from ingredients on hand, and many provide a delectable way to use a surplus of fruit: overripe bananas, peaches from a bountiful tree, an overabundance of strawberries during the height of strawberry season. They are also, of course, an ideal way to satisfy a sweet tooth, at breakfast or for a snack.

Baking powder and baking soda are the essential agents that cause quick breads to rise while also lightening them and imparting a pleasing texture. Both begin to react as soon as they come in contact with moisture. Today's baking powder is double-acting, that is, it does its work in two stages—first through reaction with moisture, and again with heat. Baking soda, however, reacts only with acidic liquids and begins working the instant it comes in contact with, say, buttermilk or yogurt. Frequently the best recipes contain both baking powder and soda, as well as the appropriate liquid.

All you need do to achieve perfect results with quick breads is to follow a few simple rules. You must have all the ingredients at hand before you begin. The oven must be preheated and the pan prepared. And most important, you should thoroughly mix the dry ingredients in one bowl and the liquid ingredients in another. Kept in separate bowls, they may wait almost indefinitely, but after you combine the two sets of ingredients, you must work very quickly. The liquid ingredients are poured into the dry ingredients and stirred just enough to moisten and combine them. The batter or dough must then be quickly turned into the prepared pan and popped into the oven: You want the batter to start rising in the oven, not on the countertop.

APPLE MUFFINS

Raisins, walnuts, and chunks of fresh, tart, green apples,
spiced with a dash of cinnamon and nutmeg go into these big, moist muffins
that are particularly good served slightly warm and buttered. Perfect for breakfast
or brunch, they also make a welcome accompaniment
to glazed ham, roast pork, or duck.

MAKES 1 DOZEN

1½ cups all purpose flour
2 teaspoons baking powder
¼ teaspoon baking soda
½ teaspoon salt
½ cup plus 1 tablespoon
    granulated sugar
½ teaspoon ground cinnamon
¼ teaspoon freshly grated nutmeg
    (optional)

½ cup milk
1 tablespoon lemon juice
1 large egg
4 tablespoons (½ stick) unsalted
    butter, melted and cooled
1½ cups diced (¼-inch) peeled
    green apples (2 large)
½ cup (3 ounces) raisins
½ cup (2 ounces) chopped walnuts

1. Position a rack in the center of the oven and preheat to 400°F. Line twelve 2½-inch muffin cups with paper liners or generously butter both the cups and the top surface of the muffin tin around the cups.

2. In a large bowl stir together the flour, baking powder, baking soda, salt, ½ cup of the sugar, cinnamon, and nutmeg.

3. In a medium-sized bowl stir together the milk and lemon juice to sour the milk. Whisk in the egg and melted butter. Pour this mixture all at once over the dry ingredients. Stir quickly just to partially blend the ingredients. Add the apples, raisins, and walnuts; fold together just to moisten. The batter will be thick and lumpy. Spoon it into the prepared muffin cups, dividing it equally among them. The cups will be full. Sprinkle the tops with the remaining 1 tablespoon sugar. Bake about 25 minutes. When done, the tops will spring back when lightly touched. If you have not used paper liners, loosen each muffin and tilt it on its side in the baking cup. Cool 10 to 15 minutes. If you have used paper liners, transfer the muffins right away to a rack and cool about 10 minutes. Serve warm, with butter if desired.

BLUEBERRY MUFFINS

Just about every baked glazed ham our family enjoyed
for Sunday dinner was accompanied by these scrumptious muffins. They are
equally good for breakfast or brunch.

MAKES 1 DOZEN

1¼ cups fresh blueberries
2 cups all-purpose flour
½ cup plus 1 tablespoon
   granulated sugar
1 tablespoon baking powder
¼ teaspoon baking soda
I T cinnamon   1/8 t nutmeg

½ teaspoon salt
1 large egg
1 cup buttermilk or plain yogurt
1 teaspoon vanilla extract
5 tablespoons unsalted butter, melted

1/4 c. orange juice
3/4 c. yog.
fresh/dried orange peel

1. Position a rack in the center of the oven and preheat to 400°F. Line twelve 2½-inch muffin cups with paper liners or generously butter both the cups and the top surface of the muffin pan around the cups. Rinse the blueberries and dry them on paper towels.

2. In a large mixing bowl stir together the flour, ½ cup of the sugar, baking powder, baking soda, and salt. Make a well in the center.

3. In a medium-sized bowl, whisk the egg and then whisk in the buttermilk or yogurt, vanilla, and melted butter. Pour this mixture all at once into the dry ingredients. Quickly stir just to partially blend; add the blueberries. Carefully fold together just to moisten; the batter will be thick and lumpy. Spoon it into the muffin cups, dividing it equally among them; the cups will be full. Sprinkle the tops with the remaining 1 tablespoon sugar. Bake 25 to 30 minutes. When done, the tops will spring back when lightly touched. Let cool in the pan for 5 minutes and then carefully remove and cool on a rack. If you have not used paper liners, loosen each muffin and tilt it in its cup (this prevents the bottom from becoming soggy). Cool for 10 to 15 minutes. Serve warm.

MOM'S SOUR CREAM–PEACH MUFFINS

My father planted five varieties of peaches
in our backyard in California so that we could enjoy them all summer long,
from the little white juicy ones early in the season to the big freestones later on.
I have sampled these muffins with just about every variety imaginable
and all are first-rate.

MAKES 1 DOZEN

TOPPING

¼ cup all-purpose flour
¼ cup granulated sugar
¼ teaspoon ground cinnamon

2 tablespoons unsalted butter,
softened

MUFFIN BATTER

3 medium peaches (about 4
ounces each)
1 large egg
½ cup sour cream
½ cup milk
1 teaspoon vanilla extract
4 tablespoons (½ stick) unsalted
butter, melted

2 cups all-purpose flour
½ cup granulated sugar
1 tablespoon baking powder
¼ teaspoon baking soda
¼ teaspoon salt

1. Prepare the topping: In a small bowl stir together the flour, sugar, and cinnamon; with a fork, work in the butter until crumbly. Refrigerate until needed.

2. Position a rack in the center of the oven and preheat to 400°F. Line twelve 2½-inch muffin cups with paper liners or generously butter the cups and the top of the pan around the muffin cups.

3. Bring a medium pot of water to a boil; add the peaches and blanch them for 10 to 15 seconds. Rinse under cold water and peel. Cut the peaches into ½-inch dice; you will need 1¼ cups (reserve any extra for another use).

4. In a medium-sized bowl, whisk the egg and then whisk in the sour cream, milk, vanilla, and melted butter. Stir in the diced peaches.

5. In a large bowl, stir together the flour, sugar, baking powder, baking soda, and salt. Pour in the sour cream-peach mixture all at once and stir quickly, just to moisten; the batter will be thick and lumpy. Spoon into the muffin cups, dividing it equally among them; the cups will be full. Quickly crumble the topping over the batter. Bake 25 to 30 minutes, until golden brown. The tops will spring back when lightly touched. Let cool in the pan for 5 minutes and then carefully remove and cool on a rack. If you have not used paper liners, loosen each muffin and tilt it on its side in the baking cup. Cool 10 to 15 minutes. Serve warm.

3/03 used Joy method

BANANA BREAD

We were treated to this banana bread every time bananas
in the fruit bowl became overripe. It is moist and tasty and filled with plump
golden raisins steeped in dark rum or bourbon.

MAKES ONE 9-BY-5-INCH LOAF

¾ cup (4½ ounces) golden raisins
½ cup dark rum or bourbon — *coco-*
1¾ cups all-purpose flour *nut*
2 teaspoons baking powder *Num.*
½ teaspoon baking soda
½ teaspoon salt
8 tablespoons (1 stick) unsalted
  butter, melted

¾ cup granulated sugar
2 large eggs
1 cup mashed very ripe bananas
  (2 medium)
½ cup (2 ounces) chopped walnuts
1 teaspoon vanilla extract

baked 35 minutes

1. In a medium-sized saucepan combine the raisins and rum or bourbon and bring to a boil over moderate heat. Remove from the heat and let stand for 1 hour. Drain, discarding any liquid that remains.

2. Position an oven rack in the center of the oven and preheat to 325°F. Grease a 9-by-5-inch loaf pan. In a medium-sized bowl stir together the flour, baking powder, baking soda, and salt.

3. In a large bowl combine the melted butter with the sugar and beat with an electric mixer until blended. Beat in the eggs, one at a time, then the mashed bananas. With a spoon, stir in the walnuts, vanilla, and drained raisins. Stir in the flour mixture, one-third at a time, mixing well after each addition. Turn into the prepared loaf pan and bake for 1 hour to 1 hour and 15 minutes, until a toothpick inserted in the center emerges clean. Cool in the pan on a rack. Slice thin and serve at room temperature.

DATE BREAD

The natural sweetness of the dates makes this bread particularly sweet. It is delicious as is or served with softened sweet butter or cream cheese for breakfast, brunch, or at any time with coffee or tea.

MAKES ONE 8½-BY-4½-INCH LOAF

1 cup (6 ounces) chopped pitted dates
1 cup (4 ounces) chopped walnuts
1 cup boiling water
1½ cups all-purpose flour
1 teaspoon baking soda

¼ teaspoon salt
4 tablespoons (½ stick) unsalted butter, softened
1 cup granulated sugar
1 large egg
1 teaspoon vanilla extract

1. In a medium-sized heatproof bowl combine the dates and walnuts; add the boiling water and let cool to room temperature, about 1 hour.

2. Position a rack in the center of the oven and preheat to 350°F. Grease an 8½-by-4½-inch loaf pan.

3. In a medium-sized bowl stir together the flour, baking soda, and salt.

4. In a large bowl beat the butter until fluffy. Gradually beat in the sugar. Add the egg and vanilla and beat until lightened, 1 to 2 minutes. Add the dry ingredients and beat just until blended. With a spoon, stir in the date mixture to blend. Turn into the prepared pan and bake until the bread just begins to pull away from the sides of the pan and the top springs back when lightly touched, 1 hour to 1 hour and 15 minutes. Cool in the pan on a rack for 15 minutes and then turn out and cool completely. Wrap in plastic and store overnight before serving. Cut into thin slices.

Apricot Coffee Cake

This is one of the best uses imaginable
for canned apricots. Not only is this a coffee cake you can make all year round,
it is simple to put together, too.

MAKES ONE 9-INCH ROUND CAKE

FILLING

One 17-ounce can unpeeled
  apricot halves in syrup, drained

½ cup (2 ounces) chopped walnuts
¼ cup packed light brown sugar

BATTER

1 cup all-purpose flour
½ teaspoon baking powder
¼ teaspoon salt
2 large eggs

6 tablespoons unsalted butter,
  melted
⅔ cup granulated sugar
1 teaspoon vanilla extract

1. Position a rack in the center of the oven and preheat to 325°F. Grease a 9-inch round cake pan or springform pan.

2. Prepare the filling: Place the drained apricots, cut side down, on several layers of paper towels until needed. In a small bowl combine the walnuts and brown sugar until blended.

3. Prepare the batter: In a large bowl stir together the flour, baking powder, and salt. In a medium-sized bowl, whisk the eggs. Add the melted butter, sugar, and vanilla and whisk until blended. Add to the dry ingredients and quickly stir together just until evenly blended. Pour half of the batter into the prepared pan and spread in an even layer. Arrange the apricots, cut side up, over the batter and sprinkle the walnut mixture over them. Spoon the remaining batter over the top but do not spread it in an even layer (some of the brown sugar mixture is pretty showing through).

4. Bake about 45 minutes, until golden brown and just beginning to pull away from the sides of the pan. Cool in the pan on a rack for about 15 minutes. Serve warm or at room temperature.

BLUEBERRY COFFEE CAKE

This cake has a delicate crumb texture and a crunchy pecan topping crumbled over its layer of fresh blueberries.

MAKES ONE 8-INCH SQUARE CAKE

TOPPING

⅓ cup all-purpose flour
½ cup packed light brown sugar
½ cup (2 ounces) chopped
　 pecans

½ teaspoon ground cinnamon
4 tablespoons (½ stick) unsalted
　 butter, softened

BATTER

1 cup all-purpose flour
1 teaspoon baking powder
¼ teaspoon baking soda
Pinch of salt
4 tablespoons (½ stick) unsalted
　 butter, softened

½ cup granulated sugar
1 large egg
1 teaspoon vanilla extract
½ cup sour cream
1½ cups fresh blueberries
1 teaspoon grated orange zest

1. Position a rack in the center of the oven and preheat to 350°F. Grease and flour an 8-inch square pan.

2. Prepare the topping: In a small bowl combine the flour, brown sugar, pecans, and cinnamon and cut in the butter to make a crumbly topping.

3. Prepare the batter: In a medium-sized bowl combine the flour, baking powder, baking soda, and salt; stir to mix.

4. In a large bowl combine the butter and sugar and beat with an electric mixer until blended. Add the egg and vanilla and beat until smooth, then beat in the sour cream. With a spoon, stir in the flour mixture to make a thick batter. Spread evenly in the prepared pan. Scatter the blueberries and orange zest over the batter and crumble the topping over the berries. Bake 50 to 60 minutes, until golden brown on top and a toothpick inserted into the cake but avoiding the berries emerges clean. Cool in the pan on a rack for about 30 minutes. Serve warm.

MOM'S PEACH COFFEE CAKE

I always think of this cake as the perfect way to brighten even the grayest of days. It is, of course, best made with tree-ripened fruit.

MAKES ONE 13-BY-9-INCH CAKE

TOPPING

¼ cup all-purpose flour
¼ cup packed light brown sugar
¼ teaspoon ground cinnamon

2 tablespoons unsalted butter, softened
½ cup (2 ounces) chopped walnuts

BATTER

4 large peaches (1½ pounds)
2 cups sifted cake flour
2 teaspoons baking powder
¼ teaspoon salt
12 tablespoons (1½ sticks) unsalted butter, softened

¾ cup granulated sugar
3 large eggs
1 teaspoon grated lemon zest
⅔ cup milk
⅓ cup packed light brown sugar
1 teaspoon ground cinnamon

1. Adjust a rack to the center of the oven and preheat to 350°F. Grease and flour a 13-by-9-inch pan.

2. Prepare the topping: In a small bowl combine the flour, brown sugar, and cinnamon and cut in the butter to make a crumbly topping. Stir in the walnuts.

3. Prepare the batter: Bring a medium-sized pot of water to a boil; add 2 peaches, and blanch 10 to 15 seconds. Remove with a slotted spoon and rinse under cold water. Repeat with the remaining peaches. Peel, halve, pit, and cut into ½-inch slices.

4. In a medium-sized bowl stir together the cake flour, baking powder, and salt.

5. In a large bowl combine the butter and granulated sugar and beat with an electric mixer until well blended. Beat in the eggs, one at a time, and then the lemon zest. Beat in the milk alternately with the flour mixture, about one-fourth at a time, beginning and ending with milk. The batter will be thick and fluffy.

6. In a small bowl combine the brown sugar with the cinnamon. Spread half the batter evenly in the prepared pan. Arrange all of the peaches over the batter and sprinkle with the brown sugar-cinnamon mixture. Spread the remaining batter evenly over the top, pushing in any peaches that are not completely covered. Crumble the topping over the batter and bake about 40 minutes. When done, a toothpick inserted into the cake above the layer of peaches will emerge clean and the cake will begin to pull away from the sides of the pan. Cool in the pan on a rack. Cut into squares and serve warm or at room temperature.

NECTARINE KUCHEN

This refreshingly simple coffee cake is rich and moist.
We often had it for Sunday morning breakfast to make use of the colorful fruit from a reliable old tree in the backyard.

MAKES ONE 9-INCH ROUND CAKE

3 cups ¾-inch slices unpeeled
   nectarines (6 medium)
2 tablespoons fresh lemon juice
1¼ cups all-purpose flour
½ cup granulated sugar
2 teaspoons baking powder

½ teaspoon salt
2 large eggs
2 tablespoons milk
1 tablespoon grated orange zest
4 tablespoons (½ stick) unsalted
   butter, melted

TOPPING

¼ cup granulated sugar
½ teaspoon ground cinnamon
½ teaspoon grated nutmeg

2 egg yolks
⅓ cup heavy cream

1. Position a rack in the center of the oven and preheat to 400°F. Grease a 9-inch springform pan. In a medium-sized bowl, toss together the nectarine slices and lemon juice.

2. In a medium-sized bowl stir together the flour, sugar, baking powder, and salt. In a large bowl whisk together the eggs, milk, and orange zest and then whisk in the melted butter. Stir in the dry ingredients and mix until smooth, then turn the batter into the prepared pan. Drain the nectarine slices and, beginning around the edge, arrange them in an overlapping layer to completely cover the top.

3. Prepare the topping: In a small bowl combine the sugar, cinnamon, and nutmeg and sprinkle over the nectarines. Bake for about 35 minutes, until a toothpick inserted in the cake between the nectarine slices emerges clean. Remove from the oven. In a small bowl stir together the egg yolks and cream; pour over the kuchen and bake 10 minutes longer, until set. Cool in the pan on a rack for 10 minutes. Run a knife around the edge and remove the pan sides. Cool about 15 minutes longer, then cut into wedges and serve warm.

PLUM COFFEE CAKE

The recipe for this special coffee cake was handed down
from my great-great-grandmother, Fanny Drabek Huletz, from Austria.
Easy to prepare, this cake has a delightfully fresh flavor.

MAKES ONE 8-INCH SQUARE CAKE

1 cup all-purpose flour
1 teaspoon baking powder
¼ teaspoon salt
8 tablespoons (one stick) unsalted
  butter, softened
⅓ cup granulated sugar
½ teaspoon grated lemon zest

¼ teaspoon grated nutmeg
2 large eggs
1½ cups ½-inch slices unpeeled
  pitted red or purple plums
  (4 medium)
¼ cup packed light brown sugar

1. Position a rack in the center of the oven and preheat to 350°F. Grease and flour an 8-inch square pan.

2. In a medium-sized bowl stir together the flour, baking powder, and salt. In a medium-sized bowl combine the butter, granulated sugar, lemon zest, and nutmeg and beat with an electric mixer until fluffy. Beat in the eggs one at a time. Add the dry ingredients and beat just until evenly blended. Turn into the prepared pan. Arrange the plum slices closely together all over the batter, pushing them halfway in. Sprinkle the brown sugar over the plums and bake 30 to 35 minutes, until golden brown. When cake is done, a toothpick inserted between the slices of plum will emerge without crumbs clinging. Cool in the pan on a rack at least 15 minutes. Cut into squares and serve warm.

SOUR CREAM–PEAR COFFEE CAKE

Anyone who likes pears should try this simple coffee cake.
Despite the long list of ingredients, it is not hard to prepare, and can be made
a day ahead of time. The sour cream provides a welcome balance to the rich
and moist cake, while the cinnamon and walnuts add flavor and texture.

MAKES ONE 9-INCH ROUND CAKE

FILLING AND TOPPING

2 tablespoons unsalted butter,
 softened
¼ cup all-purpose flour
¼ cup granulated sugar

1 teaspoon ground cinnamon
½ cup (2 ounces) chopped
 walnuts

BATTER

4 tablespoons (½ stick) unsalted
 butter
1½ cups all-purpose flour
½ cup granulated sugar
1 teaspoon baking powder
½ teaspoon baking soda
½ teaspoon salt

2 large eggs
½ cup sour cream
1 teaspoon vanilla extract
3 medium Bosc pears
 (about 1 pound)
1 tablespoon lemon juice

GLAZE

½ cup sifted confectioner's sugar
1 tablespoon unsalted butter,
 softened

½ teaspoon vanilla extract
2 teaspoons milk

1. Line a 9-inch round cake pan with aluminum foil and grease and flour the foil;
or grease and flour a 9-inch springform pan. Position a rack in the center of the
oven and preheat to 375°F.

2. Prepare the filling and topping: In a small bowl combine the butter, flour, sugar,
and cinnamon; rub together with your fingers or stir with a fork until the butter
moistens the other ingredients. Stir in the walnuts.

3. Prepare the batter: Melt the butter in a small saucepan or skillet and set aside to cool slightly. In a large bowl stir together the flour, sugar, baking powder, baking soda, and salt.

4. In a medium-sized bowl whisk the eggs until blended. Whisk in the sour cream, vanilla, and melted butter.

5. Using a swivel-bladed vegetable peeler, peel the pears, then halve them length-wise. Use a pear corer or melon baller to scoop out the cores from the center, then cut out the fiber that runs to the stem and to the bottom. Cut the pears lengthwise into ½-inch slices.

6. Whisk the egg mixture once more and turn into the dry ingredients. Stir just to blend evenly. Spread half of the batter in the prepared pan. With wet fingertips, pat the batter to the edges of the pan. Sprinkle with half of the filling and topping mixture. Spoon the remaining batter over and, with wet fingertips, pat in an even layer. Arrange the pear slices, slightly overlapping or fanning them, in a circle on the top; fill in the center with any remaining slices to make a mound. Brush with the lemon juice and sprinkle with the remaining filling and topping mixture. Bake 40 to 45 minutes, until the sides just begin to pull away from the pan sides and a toothpick inserted into the cake between slices of pear comes out crumb-free. Cool in the pan on a rack for 20 minutes.

7. Meanwhile, make the glaze: In a small bowl combine the confectioner's sugar and butter and stir together until the butter is worked into the sugar. Stir in the vanilla and milk to make a smooth glaze.

8. Loosen the cake from the pan and carefully turn out onto a plate (or onto your hand) and invert so the cake is right side up on a serving plate. With a spoon or with a pastry bag fitted with a small plain tip, drizzle the glaze in squiggles all over the top. Serve slightly warm or at room temperature.

ORANGE COFFEE CAKE

This simple coffee cake has a refreshing orange flavor
and is easy to prepare. When we lived in California our family enjoyed it often,
making wonderful use of the plump juicy oranges
from the trees in our backyard.

MAKES ONE 8-INCH SQUARE CAKE

TOPPING

½ cup (2 ounces) chopped
   walnuts or pecans
¼ cup all-purpose flour
¼ cup granulated sugar

2 tablespoons unsalted butter,
   chilled
1 tablespoon grated orange zest
1 teaspoon ground cinnamon

BATTER

4 tablespoons (½ stick) unsalted
   butter
1 cup all-purpose flour
¼ cup granulated sugar
1 teaspoon baking powder

1 tablespoon grated orange zest
Pinch of salt
½ cup fresh orange juice
1 large egg, slightly beaten
1 teaspoon vanilla extract

1. Position a rack in the center of the oven and preheat to 400°F. Grease an 8-inch square pan.

2. In a small bowl combine the nuts, flour, sugar, butter, orange zest, and cinnamon; with a pastry blender or your fingers, work in the butter until the mixture is crumbly.

3. Prepare the batter: Melt the butter in a small pan over low heat. In a medium-sized bowl stir together the flour, sugar, baking powder, orange zest, and salt. Make a well in the center and add the orange juice, egg, vanilla, and melted butter; stir just until evenly moistened and turn into the prepared pan. Crumble the topping over the batter and bake about 30 minutes, until a toothpick inserted in the center emerges clean. Cool on a rack for about 15 mintues, then cut into squares and serve warm.

DANISH PUFF COFFEE CAKE

As if by magic, the top layer of this coffee cake puffs up and collapses during baking, creating dozens of flaky, moist layers. The resulting cake is reminiscent of Danish pastry, without the complicated work. When glazed and topped with slivered almonds and confectioner's sugar, it is very professional-looking indeed.

MAKES TWO 12-BY-3-INCH CAKES

BOTTOM LAYER

8 tablespoons (1 stick) unsalted butter, softened
1 cup all-purpose flour

Pinch of salt
2 tablespoons ice water

TOP LAYER

8 tablespoons (1 stick) unsalted butter, sliced
1 cup milk
1 cup all-purpose flour

3 tablespoons granulated sugar
½ teaspoon almond extract
3 large eggs

GLAZE

1½ cups sifted confectioner's sugar
2 tablespoons unsalted butter, softened

1½ teaspoons vanilla extract
1 tablespoon milk

TOPPING

¾ cup (3 ounces) slivered blanched almonds

1 tablespoon confectioner's sugar

1. Position a rack in the center of the oven and preheat to 350°F. Have ready an ungreased baking sheet.

2. Prepare the bottom layer: In a medium-sized bowl cut the butter into the flour until it resembles coarse meal. With a fork stir in the salt and the ice water to make a soft dough.

3. Divide the dough in half. Shape one half into a 6- to 8-inch rope and place on one half of the baking sheet. With your fingers, pat out the dough to make a long rectangle that measures 12 by 3 inches (a ruler can be pressed along the sides to make them straight). Repeat with the second piece of dough on the same sheet. Refrigerate until needed.

4. Prepare the top layer: In a heavy medium-sized saucepan combine the butter and milk; bring just to the boil over moderate heat. Remove from the heat and add all of the flour, the sugar, and the almond extract; stir vigorously with a wooden spoon until the mixture forms a ball. Beat in the eggs one at a time, beating thoroughly with the spoon after each addition. Spread half of this mixture evenly over each chilled dough rectangle to make a thick layer. Bake 50 to 60 minutes, until puffy and golden brown all over. Cool for 10 minutes and then spread with the glaze. Leave the oven on.

5. Prepare the glaze: In a medium-sized bowl combine the confectioner's sugar and butter; stir together until the butter is worked into the sugar. Stir in the vanilla and milk to make a smooth glaze. Spread over the baked rectangles.

6. Prepare the topping: Place the slivered almonds on a baking sheet and toast in the 350°F oven for about 10 minutes, tossing them once or twice, until golden brown. Immediately scatter over the glaze, using half for each coffee cake. The coffee cakes are good served slightly warm or at room temperature. Before serving, sift the confectioner's sugar over the top. Slice crosswise.

Walnut Coffee Cake

A wonderfully moist, comforting cake,
splendid with a cup of good coffee. The center is filled with two layers of ground walnuts flavored with cinnamon and vanilla.

MAKES ONE 10-INCH BUNDT CAKE

FILLING

1½ cups (6 ounces) walnuts
½ cup packed light brown sugar
1 tablespoon vanilla extract

1½ teaspoons ground cinnamon
1 tablespoon heavy cream or milk

BATTER

2¾ cups all-purpose flour
1½ teaspoons baking powder
1½ teaspoons baking soda
½ teaspoon salt
10 tablespoons (1¼ sticks)
   unsalted butter, softened

1 cup granulated sugar
2 teaspoons vanilla extract
3 large eggs
2 cups sour cream
1 tablespoon confectioner's sugar,
   for topping

1. Prepare the filling: In the container of a food processor or blender, combine the walnuts, brown sugar, vanilla, cinnamon, and cream; process until coarsely ground.

2. Adjust a rack to the center of the oven and preheat to 350°F. Grease a 10-inch Bundt pan and lightly flour, tapping out the excess.

3. Prepare the batter: In a medium-sized bowl, combine the flour, baking powder, baking soda, and salt; stir together and then sift into another bowl or onto waxed paper.

4. In a large bowl, beat the butter with an electric mixer until fluffy. Gradually beat in the sugar, then the vanilla and the eggs, one at a time. At low speed, beat in the flour mixture alternately with the sour cream, beginning and ending with the flour mixture, to make a thick, smooth batter.

5. Spread one-third of the batter in the prepared pan. Sprinkle with half of the filling and spread with half of the remaining batter; sprinkle with the remaining filling and spread with the remaining batter. Bake for 55 to 60 minutes, until the top springs back when lightly touched and a toothpick inserted emerges clean. Cool in the pan on a rack for 10 minutes. Invert onto a serving plate and cool about 15 minutes more. Sift the confectioner's sugar over the top, then cut into slices and serve warm.

CINNAMON CAKE

Very light and moist, this coffee cake makes a good addition to breakfast or brunch. It has a wonderful cinnamon flavor and aroma.

MAKES ONE 8- OR 9-INCH SQUARE CAKE

1 ½ cups all-purpose flour
1 teaspoon baking soda
¼ teaspoon baking powder
¼ teaspoon salt
8 tablespoons (1 stick) unsalted butter, softened
¾ cup granulated sugar

2 large eggs
1 teaspoon vanilla extract
1 cup sour cream
½ cup (2 ounces) finely chopped pecans
4 teaspoons ground cinnamon

1. Position a rack in the center of the oven and preheat to 350°F. Grease an 8- or 9-inch square pan.

2. In a medium-sized bowl stir together the flour, baking soda, baking powder, and salt.

3. In a large bowl combine the butter with ½ cup of the sugar; beat with an electric mixer until blended. Beat in the eggs, one at a time, and then the vanilla. Beat in half of the dry ingredients just until blended. Beat in the sour cream and then the remaining dry ingredients. Stir in the pecans. In a small bowl stir together the remaining ¼ cup sugar and the cinnamon. After turning the batter into the pan, spoon the cinnamon-sugar evenly over the top and use a butter knife to swirl the mixture down into the batter for a marbled effect. Bake 30 to 35 minutes, until the top springs back when lightly touched and a toothpick inserted in the center emerges clean. Cool in the pan on a rack for 15 minutes, then cut into squares and serve warm.

IRISH SODA BREAD

My mother often made this soda bread
the night before she wanted to serve it. The next morning it was sliced and
toasted and served with soft sweet butter; the toast has a crispy surface texture
and is even crunchier than toasted English muffins.

MAKES ONE 8-INCH ROUND LOAF

3½ cups all-purpose flour
¼ cup granulated sugar
1 teaspoon baking powder
½ teaspoon baking soda
½ teaspoon salt
½ cup raisins

2 tablespoons whole caraway
    seeds
4 tablespoons (½ stick) unsalted
    butter, softened
1½ cups buttermilk

1. Position a rack in the center of the oven and preheat to 350°F. Grease an 8-inch round cake pan.

2. In a large bowl stir together the flour, sugar, baking powder, baking soda, salt, raisins, and caraway seeds. Add the butter and work it in with your fingertips just until blended. Add the buttermilk and stir quickly, just until evenly moistened, to make a sticky dough. Turn the dough into the prepared pan and pat into an even layer. Dip a sharp knife into flour and score a large X over the top to mark dough about ¼ inch deep and in even quarters. Bake about 1 hour, until golden brown; a toothpick inserted in the center will come out clean. Turn the bread out, wrap it in a linen towel, and cool it for 6 hours or overnight. You can break the loaf along the farls (the Irish word for quarters) if desired, and then cut it into ½- or ¾-inch slices and toast. Serve hot with sweet butter.

❧ YEAST BREADS ❧

When I was a boy, the ritual of making yeast bread always began with my mother's putting a kettle of water on to boil to warm the kitchen. She also warmed the bowls in which the dough would rise and the small crock in which warm water, sugar, and yeast were stirred together and then left on the kitchen table until the yeast had foamed up and doubled in size. This proofing determined whether the yeast was active or fresh enough to make the bread rise; if it was not, she'd start over with fresh yeast.

The old-fashioned method by which my mother made bread each week (most often, the nisua on page 130) continued with her use of a wooden spoon to stir up a batter of flour, milk, and melted butter—called a "sponge"—in an immense cream-colored bowl. The sponge was allowed to rise until it had doubled in bulk, at which point she stirred in more flour to make a soft, sticky dough that was kneaded on a floured board for at least ten minutes, until it was smooth and satiny and elastic. The dough was then placed gently in a buttered bowl, turned once to grease the top, then allowed to rise again.

Nowadays the process of making bread is simpler. I don't have to be concerned about heating the kitchen or the bowls, and a turned-off gas oven is a good place to let my bread rise. The fresh cakes of yeast that my mother and grandmother used are no longer widely available, and the packets of active dry yeast used for testing these recipes are less perishable and more reliable (although I still like to proof them, as described in the recipe instructions). But I do hold with some of the old ways. Like my mother, I wrap cardamom seeds in a linen napkin and pound them with a hammer to produce the wonderful fragrance of loaves spiced with ground cardamom; my grandmother used a brick to pound hers. You may of course use a spice grinder or mortar and pestle for this process, but I'll keep to the old way: It is more faithful to the ancient art of baking bread, and certainly more fun.

STICKY CARAMEL-PECAN ROLLS

Here is the ultimate recipe for classic sticky buns.
It is probably a little sweeter than most of the other recipes in this book, but that's
how these rolls are meant to be. I did reduce the amount of sugar in the dough,
but the gooey topping is still wonderfully sweet.

MAKES 1½ DOZEN

¾ cup milk
4 tablespoons (½ stick) unsalted
   butter
¼ cup granulated sugar
½ teaspoon salt

¼ cup warm (105° to 115°F) water
One ¼-ounce package active dry yeast
2 large eggs, at room temperature
4 to 4¼ cups all-purpose flour

TOPPING

1 cup packed dark brown sugar
8 tablespoons (1 stick) unsalted butter

¼ cup dark corn syrup
¾ cup (3 ounces) chopped pecans

FILLING

¾ cup (3 ounces) chopped
   pecans

½ cup packed dark brown sugar
1 tablespoon ground cinnamon

1. In a small heavy saucepan combine the milk, butter, 3 tablespoons of the sugar, and the salt; place over moderate heat and warm to 105° to 115°F; remove from the heat. If liquid should become too warm, let cool slightly to the correct temperature.

2. In a small bowl or a cup combine the remaining tablespoon of sugar with the warm water. Sprinkle the yeast over the surface and let soften for a minute; stir to dissolve and let proof until foamy, about 5 minutes.

3. In a large mixer bowl combine the eggs, milk mixture, proofed yeast, and 2 cups of the flour. Beat with an electric mixer for 2 minutes. Work in enough of the remaining flour to make a soft, slightly sticky dough. Knead on a lightly floured surface until smooth and elastic, about 10 minutes. Place in a lightly oiled bowl, turning the dough once to oil the top; cover with a clean towel or with plastic wrap and place in a warm draft-free place until doubled in size, 1 to 1½ hours.

4. Lightly grease two 9-inch round cake pans. Then prepare the topping: In a heavy medium-sized saucepan combine the brown sugar, butter, and corn syrup. Place over moderate heat and bring to a boil, stirring frequently to dissolve the sugar. Remove from the heat, stir in the pecans, and divide between the two cake pans, spreading mixture evenly over the bottoms.

5. When the dough has risen, punch it down, knead briefly, and let rest for 5 minutes.

6. Meanwhile, prepare the filling: In a small bowl stir together the pecans, brown sugar, and cinnamon.

7. On a lightly floured surface, roll the dough out into an 18-by-15-inch rectangle. Sprinkle the filling evenly over the dough. Starting with one 18-inch side, tightly roll up jelly roll style. Cut into 1-inch slices. Place one slice in the center of each prepared pan and 8 around the sides (9 per pan). Cover and let rise until almost doubled in size, about 45 minutes.

8. Meanwhile, position a rack in the lower half of the oven and preheat to 375°F. Bake rolls 25 to 30 minutes, until golden brown and hollow-sounding when tapped. Cool in the pans for 5 minutes. Run a knife around the edge and turn out, nut side up, onto serving plates, spooning any caramel and nuts that might remain in the pan on top of the rolls. Cool slightly. Serve warm or at room temperature. The rolls will pull apart.

CINNAMON ROLLS

The aroma of these old-fashioned rolls baking in the oven will make even the most stubborn of sleepyheads get out of bed. This recipe makes two dozen good-sized rolls so there will be plenty for everyone.

MAKES 2 DOZEN 3-INCH ROLLS

1 cup milk
4 tablespoons (½ stick) unsalted
  butter, sliced
½ cup granulated sugar
1 cup warm (105° to 115°F) water

Two ¼-ounce envelopes active
  dry yeast
2 large eggs, at room temperature
6 to 7 cups all-purpose flour

FILLING

¾ cup granulated sugar
4 teaspoons ground cinnamon

4 tablespoons (½ stick) unsalted
   butter, melted

GLAZE

3 tablespoons unsalted butter,
   softened
2 cups sifted confectioner's sugar

¼ teaspoon ground cinnamon
1½ teaspoons vanilla extract
2 to 3 tablespoons milk

1. Pour the milk into a small saucepan and add the butter. Reserve 1 tablespoon of the ½ cup sugar and add the remainder to the milk. Heat over low heat, stirring occasionally, until the butter melts; remove from the heat and test the temperature. If liquid is hotter than 110°F, let it cool to about that temperature.

2. Place the reserved tablespoon of sugar in a small bowl and add the warm water, stirring once or twice. Sprinkle both packages of yeast over the surface and let soften for a minute. Stir to dissolve and let proof until foamy, about 5 minutes.

3. Whisk the eggs in a large mixing bowl and whisk in the proofed yeast and the warm milk mixture. Beat in 3 cups of the flour all at once. Then beat in enough of the remaining flour to make a soft sticky dough. Turn out onto a lightly floured surface and knead until soft and elastic, about 10 minutes. Place in a lightly oiled bowl, turning the dough once to oil the top. Cover with a clean towel or with plastic wrap and let rise in a warm draft-free place until doubled in bulk, about 1 hour. Grease two 13-by-9 inch baking pans.

4. Punch the dough down and turn out onto a lightly floured surface; knead a few times, cover, and let rest 5 minutes. Cut the dough in half. With your hands, put one half into a rectangle that measures 12 by 9 inches. Repeat with the other half.

5. Prepare the filling: In a small bowl stir together the sugar and cinnamon. The melted butter should be cooled slightly. Brush half of the melted butter over each rectangle of dough. Sprinkle half of the cinnamon sugar over each. Starting with one 9-inch side, tightly roll up one piece, jelly roll style, and place seam side down. Repeat with the second piece. Cut each roll into 12 equal slices and arrange the slices, one cut side down, in the two prepared pans. Cover and let rise until almost doubled in size, about 45 minutes.

6. Meanwhile, evenly space two racks in the oven and preheat to 400°F. Uncover the rolls and bake them for 30 to 35 minutes, switching the position of the pans halfway through the baking, until golden brown. The rolls will sound hollow when tapped with a finger. Turn out onto a rack, turn the rolls right side up, and glaze while hot.

7. Prepare the glaze: In a medium-sized bowl combine the butter, confectioner's sugar, and cinnamon; work together with a spoon until blended. Stir in the vanilla and 2 tablespoons of the milk. Stir in as much more milk as needed to make a smooth glaze with a good spreading consistency. Spread over the hot rolls and let them cool for about 15 minutes. Serve warm.

SUGAR-COATED DATE TWISTS

My mother brought this recipe home
from one of our family trips to Indio, California, for the annual date festival.
I still remember our parking the car in among the groves of immense date trees,
in the shade of the giant palms. These sugar-coated twisted rolls, layered
with a moist and naturally sweet date filling,
have an unexpectedly crisp topping.

MAKES 1½ DOZEN

¾ cup milk
4 tablespoons (½ stick) unsalted
  butter
1 teaspoon salt
¼ cup granulated sugar

¼ cup warm (105° to 115°F) water
One ¼-ounce package active dry yeast
1 large egg, at room temperature
3¼ to 3¾ cups all-purpose flour

FILLING

1½ cups packed chopped pitted
  dates (9–10 ounces)
⅓ cup packed dark brown sugar
½ cup water
1 cup (4 ounces) chopped walnuts

2 tablespoons unsalted butter
2 tablespoons lemon juice
1 teaspoon vanilla extract

COATING

1 large egg   2 tablespoons granulated sugar

1. In a small saucepan combine the milk, butter, salt, and 3 tablespoons of the sugar; warm over moderate heat until liquid reaches 105° to 115°F. If it should become warmer, cool to the correct temperature.

2. In a small bowl or cup combine the warm water with the remaining 1 tablespoon sugar; sprinkle the yeast over the surface and let soften for a minute. Stir to dissolve and let proof until foamy, about 5 minutes.

3. In a large mixer bowl combine the egg with the milk mixture and proofed yeast and 2 cups of the flour; beat with an electric mixer for 2 minutes. Work in enough additional flour to make a soft, slightly sticky dough. Knead on a lightly floured surface or with a dough hook until smooth and elastic, about 10 minutes. Turn dough into an oiled bowl, flip over so the top is oiled, cover with a clean towel or plastic wrap, and set in a warm draft-free spot to rise until doubled in bulk, about 1 to 1½ hours.

4. Meanwhile, prepare the filling: In a heavy medium saucepan combine the dates and brown sugar with ½ cup of water; bring to a boil over moderate heat. Reduce the heat, cover, and simmer for about 5 minutes. Uncover and simmer, stirring frequently, until very thick, about 5 minutes longer. Remove from the heat; stir in the walnuts, butter, lemon juice, and vanilla. Cool to room temperature.

5. Punch the dough down, knead it briefly, and let rest 5 minutes. Grease two baking sheets. On a lightly floured surface, roll the dough out into a rectangle that measures 18 by 12 inches. Spread the date filling over the entire surface. Fold one 18-inch side up one-third over the filling and fold the other 18-inch side up over the first fold; this creates an 18-inch-long strip about 4 inches wide consisting of 3 layers of dough separated by date filling. Cut crosswise into 18 1-inch strips. As you place each strip on the baking sheets, twist it twice. Leaving about 2 inches between them, place 9 twists on each sheet. Cover and let rise until almost doubled in size, about 30 minutes.

6. Meanwhile, position a rack in the lower half of the oven and another in the center; preheat to 375°.

7. Coat the twists: In a small bowl stir the egg with a fork until blended. Brush the twists, with the egg and sprinkle with the sugar. Bake the twists 15 to 20 minutes, reversing the position of the sheets halfway through baking so the twists brown evenly. When they are golden brown and hollow-sounding when tapped, remove and cool on the sheets for 3 to 5 minutes; then transfer with a spatula to a rack. Serve warm.

BLACKBERRY SWIRLS

Homemade blackberry jam is what my mother always used
in these delicious coffee rolls. I have also made this recipe with a good brand
of commercially prepared blackberry jam, and the results are superb.

MAKES 2 DOZEN

¾ cup milk
8 tablespoons (1 stick) unsalted
butter, sliced
½ teaspoon salt
¼ cup granulated sugar
4 ounces (half an 8-ounce
package) cream cheese, cut up

¼ cup warm (105° to 115°F)
water
One ¼-ounce package active dry
yeast
1 large egg
3¾ to 4¼ cups all-purpose flour

FILLING

¾ cup blackberry jam or
preserves

¾ cup (3 ounces) finely chopped
walnuts

GLAZE

1½ cups sifted confectioner's sugar
2 tablespoons unsalted butter,
softened

4 teaspoons milk
1 teaspoon vanilla extract

1. In a heavy medium-sized saucepan combine the milk, butter, salt and 3 table-spoons of the sugar. Place over low heat and, stirring occasionally, warm to 105°F to 115°F. If it becomes hotter, cool enough to correct the temperature before using. Remove from the heat and stir in the cream cheese (do not attempt to melt it in; this step is only to warm it).

2. Place the remaining tablespoon of sugar in a small bowl or a cup. Stir in the warm water and sprinkle the yeast over the surface; let soften for about a minute and then stir to dissolve. Let proof until foamy, about 5 minutes.

3. In a large mixer bowl combine the egg, milk mixture, and proofed yeast; add 2 cups of flour and beat with an electric mixer for 2 minutes. Work in enough of the remaining flour to make a soft, slightly sticky dough. On a lightly floured surface, knead until smooth and elastic, about 10 minutes. Place in a lightly oiled bowl, turning once to oil the top of the dough. Cover with a clean towel or with plastic wrap and let rise in a warm draft-free place until doubled in size, 1 to 1½ hours. Punch dough down, knead briefly, and let rest for 5 minutes.

4. Prepare the filling: In a small bowl stir together the jam and walnuts.

5. Grease two baking sheets. Divide the dough in half. On a lightly floured surface, roll out half of the dough into an 18-by-12-inch rectangle. Spread with half of the filling, leaving a ½-inch border all around. Starting with one 18-inch side, roll up tightly, jelly roll style. Using a ruler and a knife, lightly mark the dough at 1½-inch intervals. Using kitchen scissors and starting ¾-inch from one end, cut *almost* through the dough; then cut all the way through at the 1½-inch mark to make the first roll. Repeat. Pick up each roll and place it with one cut side down, spreading the upper part half over the lower part and half onto the sheet. Arrange rolls in 3 rows of 4 on the baking sheet. Repeat with the remaining dough and filling. Cover and let rise until almost double in size, about 45 minutes.

6. Meanwhile, position one rack in the lower half of the oven and another in the center; preheat to 375°F. Bake the rolls for about 15 minutes, switching the sheets halfway through baking if one sheet is browning more quickly than the other, until golden brown. Transfer to a rack and let cool for a few minutes before glazing.

7. Prepare the glaze: In a medium-sized bowl combine the confectioner's sugar and butter; stir together until the butter is worked into the sugar. Stir in the milk and vanilla to make a smooth glaze with a good spreading consistency. With a small spatula, spread the glaze over the hot rolls, or fill a pastry bag with a small plain tip and drizzle the glaze all over the rolls. Serve warm.

BROWN SUGAR SWIRLS

A filling of brown sugar and walnuts is rolled up
within a tangy cottage-cheese yeast dough. The dough is then sliced and twisted
on the baking sheet to form golden brown double spirals.

MAKES 1½ DOZEN

4 tablespoons (½ stick) unsalted
  butter
⅓ cup granulated sugar
¼ cup warm (105° to 115°F) water
One ¼-ounce envelope active dry
  yeast

1 large egg, at room temperature
1 cup cottage cheese, at room
  temperature
½ teaspoon salt
About 3 cups all-purpose flour

FILLING

1½ cups (6 ounces) walnut pieces
¾ cup packed light brown sugar
4 tablespoons (½ stick) unsalted
  butter, sliced

1 teaspoon vanilla extract

1. Melt the butter in a small pan over low heat; cool until needed. Place 1 tablespoon of the sugar in a small bowl; add the warm water and stir once or twice. Sprinkle the yeast over the surface and let soften for a minute; stir to dissolve the yeast and let proof until foamy, about 5 minutes.

2. In a large mixer bowl combine the egg, cottage cheese, and salt; beat with an electric mixer until blended. Add 2 cups of the flour and beat for 2 minutes. Work in enough of the remaining flour to make a soft sticky dough. On a lightly floured surface, knead until smooth and elastic, about 10 minutes. Place in a lightly oiled bowl, turning once to oil the top of the dough. Cover with a clean towel or with plastic wrap and let rise in a warm draft-free place until doubled in size, about 1 hour. Punch down and knead briefly. Let rest for 5 minutes.

3. Prepare the filling: In a food processor combine the walnuts, brown sugar, butter, and vanilla; process until finely ground. (Without a food processor, grind the nuts and then stir in the remaining ingredients, using softened butter.)

4. Grease two baking sheets. On a lightly floured surface, roll the dough out into a

121

rectangle that measures 14 by 20 inches. Sprinkle all of the filling over the dough in an even layer. Starting with one 14-inch side, roll up, jelly roll fashion, just to the center. Roll up the opposite side in the same manner so the rolls meet in the center. With a sharp knife, cut the double roll crosswise into ¾-inch slices. As you place each slice on the prepared sheets (allowing room for 9 rolls on each sheet), twist half of the slice to make an "S" shape. Cover and let rise until almost doubled in size, 1 to 1½ hours.

5. Meanwhile, position two racks, one in the lower half of the oven and the other in the center; preheat the oven to 375°F. Bake the rolls about 12 minutes, until golden brown, switching the sheets halfway through baking if one is browner than the other. With a spatula, transfer to racks to cool slightly. Serve warm.

HUNGARIAN COFFEE CAKE

Delicious and elegant and fun to eat,
the rounds of rich coffee cake simply pull apart. The walnut-cinnamon topping
adds flavor and texture and holds the cake together.

MAKES ONE 10-INCH RING

1 cup milk
¼ cup granulated sugar
4 tablespoons (½ stick) unsalted
  butter

½ teaspoon salt
One ¼-ounce package active dry yeast
1 large egg, at room temperature
About 3½ cups all-purpose flour

COATING

8 tablespoons (1 stick) unsalted
  butter
1 cup (4 ounces) finely chopped
  walnuts

¾ cup granulated sugar
1 tablespoon ground cinnamon
½ cup (3 ounces) raisins

1. In a small heavy saucepan combine the milk, sugar, butter, and salt; place over low heat and warm to 105° to 115°F. (If liquid overheats, let cool until the correct temperature is reached.) Sprinkle the yeast over the surface and let soften for about 1 minute. Stir to dissolve and let proof until foamy, 3 to 5 minutes.

2. In a large mixer bowl beat the egg slightly. Add the proofed yeast mixture and 2 cups of the flour; beat with an electric mixer for 2 minutes. Beat in enough of the remaining flour to make a soft, sticky dough. Knead on a lightly floured surface until smooth and elastic, about 10 minutes. Place in a lightly oiled bowl, turning once to oil the top; cover with a clean towel or with plastic wrap and let rise in a warm draft-free place until doubled in size, about 1 hour. Punch down, knead briefly and let rest 5 minutes.

3. Meanwhile, prepare the coating: In a small skillet, melt the butter over low heat and cool slightly. In a medium-sized bowl toss together the walnuts, sugar, and cinnamon. Reserve the raisins for scattering on the layers.

4. Generously grease or butter a 10-inch tube pan (preferably one *without* a removable bottom; otherwise place the pan over a sheet of aluminum foil during baking to catch any drips). Pinch off pieces of the dough and roll them between the palms of your hands to make balls about the size of walnuts. Dip one at a time into the melted butter and then roll in the cinnamon-sugar mixture to coat generously. Place them in the prepared pan, leaving about ½ inch between the balls. When half are arranged in one layer, scatter half of the raisins over them. Repeat to make a second layer. Scatter the rest of the raisins over, followed by any remaining cinnamon-sugar. If any butter is left, spoon it over the top. Cover and let rise until almost doubled in size, about 1 hour.

5. Meanwhile, position a rack in the lower half of the oven and preheat to 375°F. Bake the coffee cake 35 to 40 minutes, until golden brown and hollow-sounding when tapped. Invert onto a serving plate, allowing any butter in the pan to run over the top. Cool 10 to 15 minutes. Serve warm.

BUTTERED ORANGE COFFEE CAKE

Soft and delicate orange rolls with a luscious, gooey glaze, these are a welcome sight on a Sunday morning.

MAKES ONE 13-BY-9-INCH COFFEE CAKE (24 ROLLS)

8 tablespoons (1 stick) unsalted butter
¾ cup granulated sugar
¼ cup warm (105° to 115°F) water
1 package (¼-oz.) active dry yeast

2 large eggs, at room temperature
½ cup sour cream, at room temperature
2¾ to 3 cups all-purpose flour

FILLING

1 cup (3 ounces) shredded sweetened coconut

½ cup granulated sugar
4 teaspoons grated orange zest

GLAZE

½ cup granulated sugar
¼ cup fresh orange juice
4 tablespoons (½ stick) unsalted butter, sliced

½ cup sour cream

1. In a small pan over low heat melt the butter and let it cool slightly. In a small bowl combine 1 tablespoon of the sugar with the warm water; sprinkle the yeast over the surface and let soften for a minute. Stir to dissolve and let proof until foamy, about 5 minutes.

2. In a large mixer bowl combine the eggs and sour cream; beat with an electric mixer until blended. Add the remaining sugar, 6 tablespoons of the melted butter (reserve 2 tablespoons), the proofed yeast mixture, and 1½ cups of the flour; beat for 2 minutes. Work in enough of the remaining flour to make a soft sticky dough. On a floured surface, knead until smooth and elastic, about 10 minutes. Place in a lightly oiled bowl, turning once to oil the top of the dough. Cover with a clean towel or with plastic wrap and let rise in a warm draft-free place until doubled in size, about 1 hour.

3. Position a rack in the center of the oven and preheat to 350°F. Prepare the filling: Sprinkle the coconut on a baking sheet and toast in the oven until light golden brown, turning once or twice, for 8 to 10 minutes. Remove and reserve ¼ cup for the topping. Place the remaining toasted coconut in a medium bowl and toss with the sugar and orange zest.

4. Punch the dough down, knead it briefly, and let it rest for 5 minutes. Grease a 13-by-9-inch baking pan. Divide the dough in half and roll out one half to a 12-inch round. Brush with 1 tablespoon of the reserved melted butter and sprinkle with half of the coconut filling. Using a knife with a long blade (or a pizza wheel), cut into 12 equal wedges. Starting at the wide end, roll up each piece and place, point side down in the prepared pan in three rows. Repeat with the remaining dough and filling, placing all 24 rolls in one pan. Cover and let rise until almost doubled in size, about 45 minutes.

5. Preheat the oven to 350°F. Uncover the rolls and bake 25 to 30 minutes, until golden brown. Remove from the oven and pour the hot glaze over the hot rolls.

6. Prepare the glaze: In a small heavy saucepan combine the sugar, orange juice, and butter; bring to a boil over moderate heat and boil for 3 minutes. Remove from the heat and stir in the sour cream. Pour all over the hot rolls and sprinkle with the reserved ¼ cup toasted coconut. Let stand for about 15 minutes, and serve warm, or cool to room temperature.

ALMOND COFFEE RING

These beautiful, intricate-looking rings
are very special, suitable for Sunday breakfast or holiday brunch. They are filled
with ground almonds and topped with a shiny glaze.

MAKES TWO 10-INCH RINGS

1 cup milk
8 tablespoons (1 stick) unsalted
 butter, sliced
⅓ cup granulated sugar
½ teaspoon salt
¼ cup warm (105° to 115°F) water

One ¼-ounce package active dry
 yeast
1 large egg, at room temperature
2 egg yolks
4 to 4½ cups all-purpose flour

FILLING

8 ounces (about 1¾ cups)
  blanched almonds
¾ cup granulated sugar
8 tablespoons (1 stick) unsalted
  butter, sliced

¼ cup milk
½ teaspoon almond extract
¼ teaspoon ground cinnamon

GLAZE

1½ cups sifted confectioner's sugar
2 tablespoons unsalted butter, softened

4 teaspoons milk
1 teaspoon vanilla extract

1. In a small heavy saucepan combine the milk and butter. Remove 1 tablespoon of the sugar and reserve for proofing the yeast; add the remaining sugar to the milk, along with the salt. Place over low heat and, stirring occasionally, warm to 105° to 115°F. (If liquid overheats, cool slightly before using.)

2. Combine the reserved tablespoon of sugar with the warm water in a small bowl. Sprinkle in the yeast and let soften for about 1 minute, then stir to dissolve. Let proof until foamy, about 5 minutes.

3. In a large mixer bowl combine the egg and egg yolks. Beat briefly and then add the proofed yeast, milk mixture, and 2 cups of the flour. Beat with an electric mixer for 2 minutes and then work in enough of the remaining flour to make a soft, slightly sticky dough. Knead on a lightly floured surface until smooth and elastic, about 10 minutes. Place in a lightly oiled bowl, turning once to oil the top of the dough. Cover with a clean towel or with plastic wrap and let rise in a warm draft-free place until doubled in size, 1 to 1½ hours. Punch down, knead briefly, and let rest 5 minutes.

4. Meanwhile, prepare the filling: In a food processor, combine the almonds, sugar, butter, milk, almond extract, and cinnamon; process until the nuts are finely ground. Without a processor, put the nuts through a grinder and then stir in the remaining ingredients.

5. Grease two baking sheets. Divide the dough in half and roll one half out to a 16-by-12-inch rectangle. Spread half (about 1 cup) of the filling over the dough. Starting with one 16-inch side, tightly roll up jelly roll fashion; pinch to seal the seam and ends. Place in a ring shape on one sheet, pinching the ends together to complete the ring. With kitchen scissors, cut straight down through the roll every ¾ inch, cutting to within ½ inch of the baking sheet (be careful not to cut all the way through). Gently separate and pull the slices alternately left and right, twisting them just enough so they lie almost flat (cut side up). Cover and let rise until almost doubled in size, 45 minutes to 1 hour. Repeat with the remaining half of the dough and filling.

6. Position the oven racks so that one is toward the bottom and the other is in the center. Preheat to 375°F. Bake the rings for about 20 minutes, reversing the sheets after 10 minutes so the browning is even, until they are golden brown and hollow-sounding when tapped. Let rest for 10 minutes and then glaze.

7. Prepare the glaze: In a medium-sized bowl combine the confectioner's sugar and butter; stir together until the butter is worked into the sugar. Stir in the milk and the vanilla to make a smooth glaze with a good spreading consistency. With a small spatula, spread the glaze over the hot rings. Serve warm or at room temperature.

APPLE–SOUR CREAM COFFEE RING

These fragrant, decorative coffee rings use a dough
very rich in butter and fortified with sour cream and egg yolks. The apple walnut
filling may be made at any time of year, but is particularly good
when the various cooking apples are harvested in the fall.

MAKES 2 RINGS

FILLING

4 large tart green cooking apples
   such as Granny Smith, greening,
   or Baldwin, 6 to 8 ounces each
1 teaspoon grated lemon zest
3 tablespoons fresh lemon juice
¾ cup granulated sugar

2 tablespoons all-purpose flour
¼ teaspoon ground cinnamon
2 egg yolks
2 tablespoons butter
1 teaspoon vanilla extract
1 cup (4 ounces) chopped walnuts

DOUGH

⅓ cup milk
1 cup (2 sticks) unsalted butter
½ cup granulated sugar
1 teaspoon salt
1 cup sour cream

¼ cup warm (105° to 115°F) water
Two ¼-ounce packages active dry yeast
4 egg yolks
5¼ to 5¾ cups all-purpose flour

127

GLAZE

1½ cups sifted confectioner's sugar
2 tablespoons unsalted butter, softened

4 teaspoons milk
1 teaspoon vanilla extract

1. Prepare the filling: Peel the apples and shred them through the coarse side of a cheese grater into a large bowl; discard the cores. Toss apple shreds with the lemon zest and lemon juice. In a heavy enameled saucepan combine the apple mixture and the sugar. Cook over moderate heat, stirring frequently, until almost boiling. Sprinkle the flour over the top and stir quickly to blend. Stir in the cinnamon and cook over moderate heat, stirring, until thickened, 2 to 3 minutes.

2. In a small bowl, stir the egg yolks. Stir in about ½ cup of the hot apple mixture and return all to the pan. Cook, stirring, until thickened further, 1 to 2 minutes. Remove from the heat and stir in the butter, vanilla, and walnuts. Cool to room temperature. (This filling can be prepared a day ahead, covered, and refrigerated, and then returned to room temperature before using.) You will have 3 cups.

3. Prepare the dough: In a heavy medium-sized saucepan combine the milk and butter. Add all but 1 tablespoon of the sugar and the salt; heat to 105° to 115°F. If liquid becomes hotter, cool to the correct temperature. Remove from the heat and stir in the sour cream.

4. In a small bowl combine the warm water with the reserved tablespoon sugar; sprinkle the yeast over the surface and let soften for a minute. Stir to dissolve and let proof until foamy, about 5 minutes.

5. In a large mixer bowl beat the egg yolks with the warm milk mixture, the proofed yeast, and 2½ cups of the flour; beat with an electric mixer for 2 minutes and then work in enough of the remaining flour to make a soft dough. On a lightly floured surface, knead the dough until smooth and elastic, about 10 minutes. Place in a lightly oiled bowl, turning once to coat both sides of the dough; cover and let rise in a warm draft-free place until doubled in size, 1 to 1½ hours. Punch down, knead briefly, and let rest 5 minutes.

6. Grease two baking sheets. Divide the dough in half. Roll one half out on a lightly floured surface to a rectangle 18 by 10 inches. Spread with half (about 1½ cups) of the filling, leaving a ½-inch border all around. Starting with one long side, roll up tightly, jelly roll fashion. Transfer to a prepared baking sheet and shape into a ring, pinching the ends together to complete the circle. With kitchen scissors, snip at 1-inch intervals about ¾ of the way through from the outside toward the center. Turn each section slightly on a cut side; cover and let rise until almost doubled in size, 30 to 45 minutes. Repeat with the remaining ingredients to make a second ring.

7. Meanwhile, position a rack in the lower half of the oven and another in the center; preheat to 375°F. Uncover the rings and bake 25 to 30 minutes, until golden brown and hollow-sounding when tapped. Cool on the sheets for a few minutes.

8. Prepare the glaze: In a medium-sized bowl combine the confectioner's sugar and butter and work together with a spoon until blended. Stir in the milk and vanilla to make a smooth glaze, then spoon or spread over the hot coffee rings. Serve warm or at room temperature.

RAISIN BREAD

This bread makes wonderful toast, but you might try it also with cream cheese or with thin slices of ham for delicious sandwiches.

MAKES TWO 8½-BY-4½-INCH LOAVES

1½ cups milk
4 tablespoons (½ stick) unsalted butter
½ cup honey
1 teaspoon salt
¼ cup warm (105° to 115°) water

1 tablespoon granulated sugar
One ¼-ounce package active dry yeast
1 large egg, at room temperature
6 to 6½ cups all-purpose flour
2 teaspoons ground cinnamon
1½ cups (9 ounces) raisins

GLAZE

1 egg yolk

1 teaspoon water or milk

1. In a medium-sized saucepan combine the milk, butter, honey, and salt; place over moderate heat and warm to 105° to 115°F. If mixture should become too warm, cool to the correct temperature.

2. In a small bowl combine the warm water and sugar. Sprinkle the yeast over the surface and let soften for a minute. Stir to dissolve the yeast and let proof until foamy, about 5 minutes.

3. In a large mixer bowl beat the egg with the milk mixture, proofed yeast, 3 cups of the flour, and the cinnamon; beat with an electric mixer for 2 minutes. Work in enough of the remaining flour to make a soft dough. Knead on a lightly floured surface until smooth and elastic, about 10 minutes (or use a mixer with a dough hook). Knead in the raisins. Place in a lightly oiled bowl, turning once to oil the top of the dough. Cover and let rise in a warm draft-free place until doubled in size, 1 to 1½ hours.

4. Meanwhile, grease two 8½-by-4½-inch loaf pans. Punch the dough down and let it rest for 5 minutes. Divide it in half and shape each into a rounded loaf; place in the pans, cover, and let rise until almost doubled in size, about 45 minutes.

5. Position a rack in the center of the oven and preheat to 400°F. In a cup, stir together the egg yolk and water. Brush over the tops of the loaves, being careful not to let the glaze run down into the pans, or bread will stick. Bake for 10 minutes; lower the oven temperature to 350°F and bake about 30 minutes longer, until the loaves are deep golden brown and hollow-sounding when thumped. Cool for a few minutes and then carefully remove. If desired, return to the oven to crisp the crust for 3 to 5 minutes. Cool on racks.

NISUA (FINNISH CARDAMOM BREAD)

No holiday gathering in our home was complete without nisua,
the aromatic Finnish cardamom bread that is braided into firm-textured,
decorative loaves. I was unable to reduce the five-loaf yield of this recipe; it simply
would not come out right. So you may want to use some of the dough
for a coffee ring with a favorite filling, as we did. Although this recipe calls
for braiding the loaves with the customary three strands of dough,
you may want to try the traditional Finnish method of using four strands.

MAKES 5 BRAIDS

One 12-ounce can evaporated milk
1 cup (2 sticks) unsalted butter
2½ cups water
2 cups granulated sugar
Two ¼-ounce envelopes active
  dry yeast

12 to 14 cups all-purpose flour
3 large eggs, at room temperature
2 teaspoons salt
1½ teaspoons ground cardamom
  seeds (from about 25 pods)

GLAZE AND TOPPING

2 egg yolks
1 teaspoon milk

2 tablespoons granulated sugar

1. In a heavy medium-sized saucepan combine the milk and butter with 2½ cups of water; place over low heat and, stirring occasionally, warm to 105° to 115°F. If liquid overheats, cool to the correct temperature. Turn into a large bowl and add 1 tablespoon of the sugar; sprinkle the yeast over the top and stir to dissolve. Stir in 4 cups of the flour to make a thin paste. Cover and let this "sponge" rise in a warm draft-free place until doubled in bulk, 30 minutes to 1 hour.

2. In a medium-sized bowl, whisk the eggs until light, 1 to 2 minutes. Add to the sponge along with the salt, cardamom, and the remaining sugar, stirring to blend. Beat in enough of the remaining flour, 1 cup at a time, beating until blended between additions, to make a soft, slightly sticky dough. Turn out onto a floured surface and knead 10 to 15 minutes, until smooth and elastic. Lightly oil a large bowl and add the dough, turning once to oil the top. Cover and let rise in a warm draft-free place until doubled in bulk, about 1½ hours.

3. Generously grease five 8-by-4-inch bread pans or two baking sheets. Punch down the dough and let it rest for 5 minutes.

4. Divide the dough into five equal parts. Working with one piece at a time, braid the dough. This can be done with four strands as the Finns do, or by using the conventional method with three ropes. To braid the Finnish way, divide one portion of the dough in half and roll each into an 18-inch rope. Cross the two ropes in the center to make an X. Bring the two upper ends forward so they are even with the other two ends (the spot where they are joined—the original X—becomes the top end of the braid). Braid the four ends by weaving them up from under and from the outside in, tucking the ends under as you complete the braid. Place it in a bread pan or on a baking sheet, and repeat with the remaining four pieces of dough. If using the conventional braiding technique, divide one portion of dough into three pieces and roll each into a 12-inch rope; pinch the top ends together and then braid with the three ropes; pinch the bottom ends together to seal and place in a bread pan, tucking the pinched ends under, or arrange the braids three across on one sheet and two on the second. Cover loosely with plastic wrap or a clean linen towel and let rise in a warm draft-free place until almost doubled in bulk, 1 to 1½ hours.

5. Evenly space two racks in the oven and preheat to 325°F about 15 minutes before the braids have completed their rise.

6. Glaze the braids: In a small bowl, lightly beat the egg yolks and milk until blended. Brush the tops of the loaves liberally with the glaze, letting it run into the crevices of the braids; sprinkle with sugar. Bake for about 45 minutes, reversing the position of the sheets after 20 minutes so that loaves brown evenly; they are done when they sound hollow when the bottoms are tapped. Cool in the pans or on the sheets for 10 minutes; remove and cool on racks. Slice and serve as is or lightly toasted, with butter.

CHRISTMAS STOLLEN

Every Christmas season we had these beautiful big sweet breads.
They are chock-full of candied cherries and citrus peel and fragrant toasted almond slivers. The top is covered in a snow white glaze and studded with cherries and nuts.

MAKES TWO 15-INCH LOAVES

1½ cups (7½ ounces) slivered
   blanched almonds
1½ cups packed (12 ounces)
   whole candied red cherries
1 cup packed (8 ounces) candied
   mixed citrus peel
½ cup (3 ounces) golden raisins
1 tablespoon brandy (optional)
1 tablespoon vanilla extract
1 cup milk

12 tablespoons (1½ sticks)
   unsalted butter, sliced
⅓ cup granulated sugar
¼ cup warm (105° to 115°F) water
Two ¼-ounce packages active dry yeast
3 large eggs, at room temperature
5½ to 6½ cups all-purpose flour
1 teaspoon grated lemon zest
½ teaspoon freshly grated nutmeg

GLAZE

1½ cups sifted confectioner's
   sugar
½ teaspoon grated lemon zest

1 tablespoon lemon juice
1 tablespoon milk

1. Position a rack in the center of the oven and preheat to 350°F. Place the almonds on a baking sheet and toast until golden, turning once, about 10 minutes. In a medium-sized bowl combine the cherries, citrus peel, raisins, brandy, and vanilla; toss together and let stand until needed. Reserve 2 tablespoons almonds and 3 whole cherries for garnish.

2. In a small saucepan combine the milk and butter. Remove and reserve 1 tablespoon of the sugar for proofing the yeast and add the remainder to the milk. Heat to between 105° to 115°F. If liquid should become too hot, cool slightly to the correct temperature.

3. In a small bowl or a cup combine the remaining tablespoon sugar with the warm water. Sprinkle the yeast over the surface and let soften for a minute. Stir to dissolve and let proof until foamy, about 5 minutes.

4. In a large mixer bowl beat the eggs just until blended. Add the milk mixture, proofed yeast, 2 cups of flour, the lemon zest, and nutmeg. Beat with an electric mixer for 2 minutes. Work in enough of the remaining flour to make a soft, slightly sticky dough. On a lightly floured surface knead until smooth and elastic, about 10 minutes. Place in a lightly oiled bowl, turning once to oil the top of the dough. Cover and let rise in a warm draft-free place until doubled in size, 1 to 1½ hours. Punch down, knead briefly, and let rest 5 minutes.

5. On a generously floured surface, pat the dough out to a large round about 1 inch thick. Add the toasted almonds and work in briefly. Add the fruit mixture and work in by kneading, pushing back in any pieces that may fall out. Divide the dough in half.

6. Grease two baking sheets. On a floured surface pat one half of the dough into an 8-by-12-inch oval. Fold in half lengthwise like an omelet, creasing the fold with the side of your hand to make sure it holds. Place on a baking sheet. Repeat with the second piece of dough. Cover and let rise until almost doubled in size, about 45 minutes.

7. Position one rack in the lower third of the oven and a second one in the center and preheat to 350°F. (If baking only one at a time, position one rack in the lower third). Bake the loaves, reversing the two sheets halfway through the baking, for 40 to 45 minutes, until golden brown and hollow-sounding when tapped.

8. Meanwhile, prepare the glaze: In a medium-sized bowl stir together the confectioner's sugar, lemon zest, lemon juice, and milk to make a smooth glaze. Spread half of it over each stollen. Before it sets, sprinkle with the reserved 2 tablespoons almonds. Halve the 3 cherries and top each loaf with 3 halves. Let glaze set. Serve warm or at room temperature.

DANISH PASTRY

Making these very special, very flaky pastries is a labor of love,
requiring several hours or a full day. Using the same procedure as for puff pastry,
you roll layers of chilled butter between layers of dough. The finished pastry
may then be used to make different kinds of individual pastries.

MAKES ENOUGH FOR 2 DOZEN INDIVIDUAL PASTRIES

1 cup milk
½ cup granulated sugar
1 teaspoon salt
¼ cup warm (105° to 115°F)
    water
Two ¼-ounce packages active dry
    yeast

2 large eggs
About 5 cups all-purpose flour
2 cups (4 sticks) unsalted butter,
    softened at cool room
    temperature for about 30
    minutes

1. Place the milk in a small saucepan. Add all but 1 tablespoon of the sugar, and the salt. Place over moderate heat and warm to 105° to 115°F. If liquid should become too hot, cool to the correct temperature.

2. In a small bowl combine the warm water with the remaining tablespoon sugar; sprinkle the yeast over the surface and let soften for a minute; stir to dissolve and let proof until foamy, about 5 minutes.

3. In a large mixer bowl beat the eggs until blended. Add the proofed yeast, the milk mixture, and 2 cups of the flour; beat with an electric mixer for 2 minutes. Work in enough of the remaining flour to make a soft dough. Knead on a lightly floured surface or with a mixer and dough hook until smooth and elastic, about 10 minutes. Place in a lightly floured bowl, turning once to flour the top, and chill in the refrigerator, covered, for about 30 minutes.

4. Meanwhile, place a 12-by-8-inch sheet of waxed paper on your work surface. Center 2 sticks of butter (just soft enough to indent with your finger) 1 inch apart on the paper and top with another sheet of waxed paper. Pound lightly with a rolling pin and then roll out to a rectangle that measures 12 by 6 inches. Repeat with the remaining 2 sticks of butter. Refrigerate until firm.

5. On a generously floured surface, roll out the dough to a rectangle that measures 18 by 12 inches. Peel the paper from one side of one sheet of butter; place, butter side down, in the center of the dough so the two 12-inch sides line up with the dough. Peel off the waxed paper and fold one end of the dough up over the butter. Brush excess flour from dough as you work. Peel one sheet of waxed paper from the other sheet of butter and center over the dough you just folded up. Peel off the waxed paper and fold the other end of the dough up over the butter; you will now have a 12-by-6-inch rectangle of dough composed of three layers of dough separated by two layers of chilled butter. Pinch to seal the edges all around, but keep the rectangle even with straight edges and corners at right angles. Dust lightly with flour, wrap in aluminum foil, and refrigerate at least 30 minutes.

6. Remove the dough from the foil and on a generously floured surface, roll out to 20 by 10 inches, keeping neat and even. Fold both 10-inch ends inward to meet in the center, brushing away excess flour. Fold in half along the line where the two ends meet; you will now have a rectangle four layers thick that measures approximately 10 by 5 inches. Return to the foil and chill for at least 30 minutes or as long as 1 or 2 hours.

7. Repeat Step 6 two more times. When done, dust with flour and wrap in aluminum foil and chill for about 3 hours or overnight. If chilling longer than 3 hours, remove and flatten occasionally, as the dough rises in the refrigerator.

Note: To make either the Raspberry-Cheese Danish (page 136) or the Bear Claws (page 137), you will need only half the dough. Prepare the entire recipe above, but cut the dough in half before proceeding, keeping the unused half refrigerated for another use.

RASPBERRY-CHEESE DANISH

MAKES 1 DOZEN

½ cup small curd cottage cheese
One 3-ounce package cream
  cheese, softened
3 tablespoons granulated sugar

½ cup raspberry jam
1 egg
2 tablespoons granulated sugar

1 egg yolk
1 teaspoon grated lemon zest
½ teaspoon vanilla extract

Half the dough for Danish Pastry
(page 134)

1. First, make the filling: Place the cottage cheese in a small sieve and let drain for 30 minutes. Turn out onto several layers of paper towels and let drain 5 minutes longer.

2. In a medium-sized bowl combine the cream cheese and sugar; beat to blend. Stir in the cottage cheese, egg yolk, lemon zest, and vanilla.

3. Butter and flour two rimmed baking sheets. On a generously floured surface, roll out the dough to a rectangle that measures 21 by 16 inches. With a sharp knife, trim the sides even to make a rectangle 15 by 20 inches. Cut into twelve 5-inch squares. Place the squares, upside down, on a floured board or sheet; chill and let rest 1 hour to relax.

4. Onto the center of each square, spoon a slightly mounded tablespoon of the cheese filling and 2 teaspoons of the jam. Bring two opposite corners up over the filling and overlap them by one inch. Place pastries 1 inch apart on the baking sheets, pressing the folds to crease them. Cover with a clean towel or plastic wrap and let rise until slightly puffy, about 30 minutes to an hour. Stir the egg in a cup and brush the pastries with this egg glaze. Sprinkle evenly with the sugar.

5. Evenly space two racks in the oven and preheat to 400°F. Place the sheets of pastries in the oven and immediately reduce the temperature to 350°F. Bake until puffy and golden brown, about 20 minutes, reversing the position of the sheets halfway through baking if they are browning unevenly. Loosen with a spatula and transfer to racks to cool. Serve just slightly warm or at room temperature.

BEAR CLAWS

MAKES 1 DOZEN

8 ounces (about 1¾ cups)
   blanched almonds
½ cup granulated sugar
4 tablespoons (½ stick) unsalted
   butter, sliced

1 large egg
2 tablespoons milk
1 teaspoon vanilla extract
¼ teaspoon almond extract

1 large egg, beaten
4 ounces (1 cup) sliced almonds
2 tablespoons granulated sugar

Half the dough for Danish Pastry
   (page 134)

1. Prepare the filling: In a food processor, combine the almonds, sugar, butter, egg, milk, vanilla, and almond extract; process until the almonds are finely ground.

2. Butter and flour two baking sheets. Cut the dough in half lengthwise and refrigerate one half. (Thus you are presently working with one-quarter of the dough from the Danish Pastry recipe.) On a generously floured surface, roll out the other half to 16 by 11 inches and with a sharp knife, trim the edges even to make a neat rectangle that measures 15 by 10 inches.

3. Working lengthwise, carefully spread half of the filling over half of the dough; Fold the other half over the filling to make a long rectangle 5 by 15 inches. Cut crosswise into six 2½-inch pieces. Working along the side of each piece opposite the fold, make 4 evenly spaced cuts three-quarters of the way through and then curve the pastries to fan the cuts as you place them on a prepared baking sheet about 2 inches apart. Remove the other half of the dough (another quarter of the original recipe) from the refrigerator and repeat the procedure, using remaining filling. Cover and let rise until puffy but not doubled in size, 30 minutes to an hour.

4. Meanwhile, evenly space two racks in the oven and preheat to 400°F. Brush the pastries with the beaten egg; sprinkle first with sliced almonds and then with the sugar. Place in the oven and immediately reduce the heat to 350°F. Bake until puffy and golden brown, about 20 minutes, reversing the position of the two sheets halfway through baking if they are browning unevenly. Loosen from the sheets with a spatula and transfer to racks to cool. Serve slightly warm or at room temperature.

❧ COOKIES AND BARS ❧

Family gatherings were made special by the incredible assortment of cookies and bars produced by my grandmother, my mother, and her four sisters: The volume and variety seemed to increase with each new holiday. I especially remember Christmastime and my mother exclaiming, "Fifty-two dozen so far this week and they're half gone already! I'd better make another batch of butter cookies."

The process of making cookies was a much-cherished ritual. From the moment I was able to sit in a high chair, I would watch my mother put on a calico apron, pull out the electric mixer (the one with a platform that spun the bowl around), and beat the eggs in a giant cream-colored bowl with a blue-striped border. She would switch to a wooden spoon to finish stirring the dough, then roll it out on the kitchen table. I'd eagerly await a taste, as well as a scrap of dough to squeeze, twist, and shape into my own creation, which my mother baked on a separate small cookie sheet. It looked soggy and gray after I'd played with the dough for a half hour or more, but it was always a masterpiece in my eyes!

The recipes in this chapter read like a roll call of favored contents for picnic baskets and brown-bag lunches, for coffee breaks and after-school snacks and general sampling from the cookie jar. From grandma's oatmeal cookies (generally acclaimed "the best I've ever tasted") to super-big chocolate chip cookies, and including peanut butter cookies, hermits (a particularly fine recipe), jumbles, sugar cookies, shortbread, and Aunt Irma's special frosted butter cookies, these are the stuff of fondest childhood memory. Likewise the bar cookies: Aunt Myra's fudge brownies; lemon bars; coconut bars; cheesecake squares; raspberry-pecan bars; and my own favorites, chocolate peanut squares, chocolate-frosted, for good measure. These are simple recipes, guaranteed to please any and all comers, year in and year out.

GRANDMA'S OATMEAL COOKIES

This is surely one of the oldest recipes in this book,
and it makes a lovely light, flavorful cookie. Whenever I'm in the mood for an old-
fashioned cookie, this is what I crave.

MAKES ABOUT 1½ DOZEN LARGE COOKIES

1½ cups old-fashioned oats
1 cup all-purpose flour
1½ teaspoons baking soda
¼ teaspoon salt
12 tablespoons (1½ sticks)
  unsalted butter, softened
¾ cup packed dark brown sugar

1 large egg
1½ teaspoons vanilla extract
1 tablespoon water
1 cup (4 ounces) coarsely
  chopped walnuts
1 cup (6 ounces) raisins

1. Position two racks so that they are evenly spaced in the oven and preheat to 350°F.

2. In a medium-sized bowl or on a large sheet of waxed paper, combine the oats, flour, baking soda, and salt; stir together.

3. In a large bowl using a handheld electric mixer set at high speed, cream the butter until fluffy, about 1 minute. Gradually add the brown sugar and beat until blended. Add the egg, vanilla, and 1 tablespoon of water; beat until thick and light, 1 to 2 minutes. Stir in the dry ingredients and the walnuts and raisins to make a thick dough.

4. Using 3 tablespoons of dough for each cookie, drop the dough onto lightly greased cookie sheets, patting to flatten slightly. Place only six cookies on each sheet and leave about 4 inches between them. Bake for 14 to 16 minutes, until lightly browned around the edges, reversing the sheets halfway through the baking, if one sheet of cookies browns sooner than the other. Let the cookies cool 2 to 3 minutes on the sheets to firm up slightly and then transfer them to absorbent paper with a spatula; let stand 5 minutes and then transfer to a rack and cool to room temperature. Use a cool baking sheet to make the rest of the cookies.

BLACK WALNUT COOKIES

The rich flavor of the black walnuts
in these delicious cookies is set off by the simple dough. No matter where she lived,
Aunt Irma always had a source for the black walnuts
to make these favorite cookies.

MAKES ABOUT 3 DOZEN

6 tablespoons (¾ stick) unsalted
   butter, softened
¾ cup packed light brown sugar
1 large egg
1 cup (4 ounces) chopped black
   walnuts

1 teaspoon vanilla extract
1¼ cups all-purpose flour
½ teaspoon salt
½ teaspoon baking soda
¼ cup milk

1. Position two racks so that they are evenly spaced in the oven and preheat to 375°F. Grease two baking sheets.

2. In a medium-sized bowl combine the butter and sugar. With a handheld electric mixer, beat until fluffy, 1 to 2 minutes. Beat in the egg until blended. With a spoon, stir in the black walnuts and vanilla.

3. On a sheet of waxed paper stir together the flour, baking powder, and salt. Stir half of the dry ingredients into the butter mixture and then stir in half of the milk. Stir in half of the remaining dry ingredients and then the remaining milk. Stir in the remaining dry ingredients to make a sticky dough.

4. Using 1 level tablespoon of the dough for each cookie, drop it onto the prepared sheets, leaving 2½ to 3 inches between them (1 dozen per baking sheet). Bake until golden brown, 8 to 10 minutes. Transfer with a spatula to a rack to cool.

CHOCOLATE CHIP COOKIES

To satisfy her four boys' love of chocolate,
my mother used to chop semisweet chocolate squares into large chunks for these
chocolate chip cookies. She made them big, just six to a baking sheet,
and they were always consumed with great quantities of milk.

MAKES ABOUT 1½ DOZEN

8 ounces (8 squares) semisweet
   chocolate or chocolate chips
1 cup all-purpose flour
½ teaspoon baking soda
8 tablespoons (1 stick) unsalted
   butter, softened
½ cup packed light brown sugar

¼ cup granulated sugar
1½ teaspoons vanilla extract
½ teaspoon salt
1 large egg
1 cup (4 ounces) chopped
   walnuts (optional)

1. Evenly space two racks in the oven and preheat to 350°F.

2. Use a sharp knife to chop the chocolate squares into large chunks. If you prefer, you can use 1⅓ cups chocolate chips.

3. On a sheet of waxed paper, stir together the flour and baking soda. In a large mixing bowl, with a handheld electric mixer, beat the butter until fluffy, about 1 minute. Add the brown sugar, granulated sugar, vanilla, and salt; beat until thick and light, 1 to 2 minutes. Beat in the egg just until blended. Using a wooden spoon, stir in the dry ingredients to make a dough. Stir in the chocolate pieces and walnuts.

4. Using about 2 tablespoons of dough for each cookie, drop the dough onto ungreased baking sheets, placing six on each sheet. Bake 10 to 12 minutes, until golden brown around the edges and only lightly colored on top. If one sheet of cookies browns sooner than the other, switch the position of the sheets halfway through baking. Let the cookies cool for 2 to 3 minutes on the sheets to firm up slightly and then transfer them to paper towels with a spatula; let stand 5 minutes, transfer to a rack and cool to room temperature. Use cool baking sheets to make cookies from the remaining dough.

Note: This dough can be prepared ahead and refrigerated for a day or two or it may be frozen.

GRANDMA'S PEANUT BUTTER COOKIES

This recipe is tried and true and very old-fashioned.
The use of cornstarch makes these especially crisp, and the crosshatch design
pressed into the top of each cookie with a fork is a sure sign
of a real peanut butter cookie.

MAKES ABOUT 3 DOZEN

1½ cups all-purpose flour
2 tablespoons cornstarch
1 teaspoon baking soda
8 tablespoons (1 stick) unsalted
   butter, softened
½ cup granulated sugar

⅓ cup packed dark brown sugar
1 large egg
¼ teaspoon salt
1½ teaspoons vanilla extract
¾ cup chunky peanut butter

1. Evenly space two racks in the oven and preheat to 350°F.

2. In a medium-sized bowl, stir together the flour, cornstarch, and baking soda.

3. In a large mixing bowl, with a handheld electric mixer, cream the butter until fluffy, about 1 minute. Gradually beat in the granulated sugar and the brown sugar. Add the egg, salt, and vanilla; beat until thick and light, 1 to 2 minutes. Beat in the peanut butter. With a wooden spoon, stir in the dry ingredients to make a moist dough that can be pressed together.

4. Using 1½ tablespoons of dough for each cookie, roll the dough into balls between the palms of your hands (they will be about 1¼ inches in diameter). Place them on ungreased baking sheets, leaving 2½ to 3 inches between them. Dip a fork in sugar and press it on top of each cookie in two directions to make a crisscross design, dipping fork back in sugar after each pressing. The cookies should be 2 inches in diameter after pressing. Bake about 12 minutes, until light golden brown around the edges. With a spatula, transfer the cookies to a rack and cool to room temperature.

DREAM COOKIES

This recipe includes potato starch along with the flour,
which in the past was a far more common baking ingredient than it is today.
These cookies are light and delicate in texture
and have a beautiful golden edge.

MAKES 3 DOZEN

1 cup (2 sticks) unsalted butter,
  softened
½ cup granulated sugar
2 tablespoons heavy cream
1 teaspoon vanilla extract

½ cup potato starch (see Note)
1 cup all-purpose flour
36 small pecan halves (about 2
  ounces)

1. Evenly space two racks in the oven and preheat to 350°F.

2. In a medium-sized bowl, with a handheld electric mixer, cream the butter; add the sugar and beat until fluffy, about 1 minute. Beat in the cream and vanilla. With a spoon, stir in the potato starch and flour.

3. Using 1 level tablespoon of dough for each cookie, drop the dough 3 inches apart onto ungreased baking sheets (12 to a sheet). Lightly press a pecan half on the top of each cookie and bake about 14 minutes, until the edges are golden brown. With a spatula, transfer to a rack and cool. Repeat with the remaining dough.

Note: Potato starch is sold in a box and is available in the kosher food section of supermarkets.

JUMBLES

A jumble of coconut and walnuts makes this an especially chewy and appealing American cookie. These drop cookies are simple to make, and they sport a shiny glaze that keeps them moist.

MAKES ABOUT 4 DOZEN

8 tablespoons (1 stick) unsalted butter, softened
½ cup granulated sugar
½ cup packed dark brown sugar
1 large egg
1 teaspoon vanilla extract
1¼ cups all-purpose flour

¼ teaspoon baking soda
¼ teaspoon salt
1 cup (3 ounces) sweetened shredded coconut
½ cup (2 ounces) chopped walnuts
½ cup sour cream

GLAZE

3 tablespoons butter
1½ cups sifted confectioner's sugar

2 tablespoons milk
½ teaspoon vanilla extract

1. Evenly space two racks in the oven and preheat to 375°F. Lightly grease two baking sheets.

2. In a large bowl, with a handheld electric mixer, beat the butter until creamy. Gradually beat in both the granulated and dark brown sugar. Add the egg and vanilla and beat until thick and light, 1 to 2 minutes. With a spoon, stir in the flour, baking soda, and salt just until blended. Stir in the coconut, walnuts, and sour cream to make a stiff dough.

3. Using 1 tablespoon of the dough for each cookie, drop onto the greased baking sheets, leaving 2 inches between cookies. Bake 10 to 12 minutes, until no impression is left when a cookie is *very* lightly touched. With a spatula, transfer the cookies to absorbent paper and immediately spread each with ½ teaspoon of the glaze. Transfer to a rack to cool.

4. While the cookies are baking, prepare the glaze: Place the butter in a small heavy skillet or saucepan over low heat. Stirring frequently, heat until deep golden brown, 3 to 4 minutes. Remove from the heat and stir in the sugar. Stir in the milk and vanilla to make a smooth glaze (it will remain shiny when spread on hot cookies).

HERMITS

Here is a lovely recipe for the cookies traditionally called hermits,
studded with raisins and chopped walnuts and scented with cinnamon. This version
also calls for a vanilla glaze. This is the quintessential cookie-with-a-glass-of-milk,
ideal for satisfying the hunger of children just home from school,
as it did mine and my brothers' on innumerable occasions.

MAKES 4 DOZEN

8 tablespoons (1 stick) unsalted
 butter, softened
¾ cup granulated sugar
1 large egg
1½ teaspoons vanilla extract
1½ cups all-purpose flour
1 teaspoon baking powder

1 teaspoon ground cinnamon
¼ teaspoon salt
¼ cup milk
1 cup (6 ounces) raisins
1 cup (4 ounces) chopped
 walnuts

GLAZE

2 tablespoons unsalted butter
1 cup sifted confectioner's sugar

1 tablespoon milk
½ teaspoon vanilla extract

1. Adjust a rack to the center of the oven and preheat to 350°F. Lightly grease a baking sheet.

2. In a large bowl beat the butter with an electric mixer until fluffy, about 1 minute. Gradually beat in the sugar. Add the egg and beat until thick and light, 1 to 2 minutes.

3. On a sheet of waxed paper stir together the flour, baking powder, cinnamon, and salt. With a spoon stir half of the dry ingredients into the butter mixture. Stir in all of the milk to blend and then stir in the remaining flour mixture. Stir in the raisins and walnuts.

4. Using 1 level tablespoon of dough for each cookie, drop the dough onto the prepared baking sheet, leaving about 2 inches between each cookie. Bake about 12 minutes, until lightly browned; when done no impression will be left on a cookie when lightly touched. Transfer to a rack.

5. While the cookies are baking, prepare the glaze: Place the butter in a small skillet over moderate heat and, stirring occasionally, cook until deep golden brown, 3 to 4 minutes. Remove from the heat and stir in about half of the sugar. Stir in the milk and vanilla and then the remaining sugar to make a smooth glaze.

6. Using about ½ teaspoon glaze for each cookie, spoon the glaze over the hot cookies. As the cookies cool, the glaze will set but remain shiny.

PECAN LACE COOKIES

Elegant enough to serve with high tea, these brittle, lacy cookies taste of caramel and toasted pecans. If your oven has a glass window, you can actually see them bubble and become lacy.

MAKES 5 DOZEN COOKIES

8 tablespoons (1 stick) unsalted butter
⅔ cup packed light brown sugar
⅓ cup light corn syrup
2 teaspoons grated orange zest

2 tablespoons orange juice
1 cup all-purpose flour
1 cup (4 ounces) finely chopped pecans

1. Adjust a rack to the center of the oven and preheat to 375°F. Line a baking sheet with a sheet of aluminum foil or lightly grease the baking sheet.

2. In a heavy medium-sized saucepan combine the butter, brown sugar, corn syrup, orange zest, and orange juice; place over moderate heat and bring to a boil. Remove from the heat and stir in the flour and pecans until evenly blended.

3. Using 1½ teaspoons of the batter for each cookie, drop it onto the prepared baking sheet, about 3 inches apart. These cookies seem to produce the best results when baking only one sheet at a time. Bake 6 to 8 minutes, until golden brown and caramelized. Carefully move the cookies, on the sheet of foil, to a rack to cool. Repeat with fresh aluminum foil. If you don't use foil, let the cookies set on the sheet for 3 minutes, then transfer to a rack to cool. If cookies stick, return them to the oven for a minute or two to resoften and then remove. Let the cookies cool to room temperature. If they are not brittle, they have not baked long enough and should be returned to the oven for a few minutes, until caramelized.

COCONUT MACAROONS

These macaroons are delicately light and airy
and have a pronounced coconut flavor. They contain only a tiny amount of flour,
just enough to hold the shreds of coconut together.

MAKES 1½ DOZEN

2 large egg whites
Pinch of salt
⅓ cup sugar
1 teaspoon vanilla extract

1½ cups (about 6 ounces) packed
    shredded sweetened coconut
3 tablespoons all-purpose flour

1. Evenly space two racks in the oven and preheat to 325°F. Butter two baking sheets.

2. In a large mixing bowl, with a handheld electric mixer, beat the egg whites and salt together until soft peaks begin to form. Gradually add the sugar and beat until stiff glossy peaks form, 1 to 2 minutes. Beat in the vanilla. Add half of the coconut and sprinkle with the flour. Add the remaining coconut and fold together carefully and thoroughly.

3. Using 2 tablespoons of the mixture for each cookie, drop onto baking sheets, leaving about 3 inches between them (place nine on each sheet). Bake 18 to 20 minutes, until light golden brown. Cool for 5 minutes and then transfer with a spatula to a rack to cool.

CARDAMOM COOKIES

These crisp and wonderful little cookies have an exotic flavor
imparted by the ground cardamom. Everyone in our family is partial to this spice,
so we use it in many of our breads and baked goods.

MAKES ABOUT 6 DOZEN

1 cup all-purpose flour
¼ teaspoon baking soda
1 teaspoon ground cinnamon
1 teaspoon ground cardamom

1 large egg
¾ cup granulated sugar
8 tablespoons (1 stick) butter,
    melted

1. Position two racks in the top two-thirds of the oven and preheat to 350°F. Grease and flour two baking sheets, tapping off the excess flour.

2. In a medium-sized bowl, stir together the flour, baking soda, cinnamon, and cardamom.

3. In a large mixing bowl whisk the egg until frothy. Whisk in the sugar and butter. With a spoon, stir in the dry ingredients.

4. Using 1 level teaspoon of batter for each cookie, drop it onto the prepared sheets about 2 inches apart. Bake 12 to 15 minutes, until lightly browned (when baking only one sheet at a time, cookies will be done in about 12 minutes). Transfer to a rack to cool. Use cooled sheets to bake the rest.

CHOCOLATE-MINT WAFERS

Crisp, thin, and delicate, these wafers are especially good with vanilla ice cream. They are best served on the day they are baked.

MAKES ABOUT 2 DOZEN COOKIES

2 ounces (2 squares) semisweet chocolate, chopped	Pinch of salt
8 tablespoons (1 stick) unsalted butter, softened	1 large egg white
½ cup granulated sugar	2 teaspoons vanilla extract
	½ teaspoon mint extract
	¾ cup all-purpose flour

1. Evenly space two racks in the oven and preheat to 350°F. Lightly butter two baking sheets. In the top of a double boiler, over hot but not simmering water, melt the chocolate. Remove the top of the double boiler from the water and cool chocolate slightly.

2. In a medium-sized bowl, combine the butter, sugar, and salt; beat with an electric mixer until blended. Add the egg white, vanilla, and mint extract and beat until smooth. Add the melted chocolate and flour and beat just until the color is even.

3. Using 1 level tablespoon of batter for each cookie, drop the cookies onto the prepared sheets, leaving 3 inches between them. Bake 12 to 14 minutes, until the edges begin to crisp. The cookies will be soft in the center but will firm up as they cool. Cool on the sheets for 1 minute. With a spatula, transfer the cookies to paper towels and cool completely. Repeat with the remaining batter.

HAZELNUT-POPPYSEED ICEBOX COOKIES

These are my grandmother's cookies, dating from the days when the iceman delivered a big block of ice on a horse-drawn cart, putting the ice through a special outside door right into her icebox. The cookies still require at least 3 hours of chilling in our modern refrigerators.

MAKES 5 DOZEN

8 ounces (1½ cups) hazelnuts
1 cup (2 sticks) unsalted butter, softened
1 cup plus 2 tablespoons granulated sugar
1 large egg
1 teaspoon vanilla extract
1 teaspoon ground ginger
2 cups all-purpose flour
½ cup whole poppyseeds

1. Preheat the oven to 350°F. Place the hazelnuts on a baking sheet and roast 10 to 12 minutes, shaking the pan once or twice to roast evenly, until the nuts are golden beneath the skins. Place the nuts in a clean towel or cloth and rub to remove the skins. It will be okay if bits of skin remain. Finely chop the nuts.

2. In a medium-sized bowl combine the butter with 1 cup of the sugar. Beat with an electric mixer until blended; beat in the egg, vanilla, and ginger. With a spoon, stir in the flour, hazelnuts, and poppyseeds to make a stiff dough. Divide the dough in half. On separate sheets of waxed paper, shape each into a rectangular log that measures 12 by 1½ by 1½ inches. Twist the ends of the paper to enclose the dough. Chill until very firm, for at least 3 hours or overnight. The logs can be stored in the refrigerator for a week or the freezer for up to 3 months.

3. Evenly space two racks in the oven and preheat to 325°F. Remove the logs from the refrigerator and coat each with 1 tablespoon of the remaining sugar, pressing it lightly to the sides so it adheres. With a sharp knife, cut the logs into ¼-inch slices and place them on ungreased baking sheets 1 inch apart. Bake 18 to 20 minutes, reversing the position of the sheets halfway through baking, or until the cookies begin to color. Transfer with a spatula to racks and cool.

CHOCOLATE-PEPPERMINT PINWHEELS

This old-fashioned icebox cookie is another
of my grandmother's recipes. The chocolate is added to half the dough, then the two
dough mixtures are layered and rolled up tightly into a log that can be made
several days ahead of time and refrigerated or frozen. When the logs
are sliced, pinwheels of chocolate and mint appear.

MAKES ABOUT 5 DOZEN

1 ounce (1 square) unsweetened chocolate	1 large egg
8 tablespoons (1 stick) unsalted butter, softened	1 teaspoon peppermint extract
1 cup granulated sugar	1½ cups all-purpose flour
	½ teaspoon baking soda
	¼ teaspoon salt

1. Melt the chocolate in the top of a double boiler over hot but not simmering water. Cool slightly.

2. In a medium-sized bowl, combine the butter and sugar and beat with a handheld electric mixer until blended. Add the egg and peppermint extract and beat until thick and light, 1 to 2 minutes. Remove half (¾ cup) of this creamed butter mixture and transfer it to another medium-sized bowl; stir in the melted chocolate. Into each of the batters stir ¾ cup of flour, ¼ teaspoon of baking soda, and ⅛ teaspoon of salt.

3. Turn out the two doughs onto separate 12-by-15-inch sheets of waxed paper. First with a spatula and then with your fingers, pat each dough into a 7-by-9-inch rectangle. Place a sheet of waxed paper over each piece of dough and lightly draw a ruler or other flat edge over the surface to smooth. Peel off the top sheets of waxed paper. Carefully turn the chocolate layer over onto the plain layer so it is evenly centered, and press the two lightly together. Peel off the top waxed paper. With the aid of the waxed paper under the bottom layer, and starting with one 9-inch side, tightly roll up, jelly roll fashion, peeling back the waxed paper as you roll. Keep the roll on the waxed paper and tightly wrap the dough in it, twisting the ends, candy-kiss fashion, in opposite directions. Refrigerate overnight (or even longer). This dough can be frozen.

4. Evenly space two racks in the oven and preheat to 375°F.

5. With a sharp knife, cut the cookie log into slices ⅙-inch thick and place them about 1 inch apart on ungreased baking sheets. Bake until golden brown, 10 to 12 minutes, reversing their position in the oven halfway through baking. Transfer with a spatula to a rack and cool to room temperature.

RUSSIAN TEA BALLS

We have always cherished the recipe for these rich,
round cookies coated in confectioner's sugar, given to my mother
by a childhood friend. To our way of thinking, no holiday cookie
assortment is complete without them.

MAKES 4 TO 5 DOZEN

1 cup (2 sticks) unsalted butter, softened
2 cups sifted confectioner's sugar
1 teaspoon vanilla extract

2¼ cups all-purpose flour
½ teaspoon salt
¾ cup (3 ounces) chopped walnuts

1. Position a rack in the center of the oven and preheat to 375°F.

2. In a large bowl combine the butter with ½ cup of the confectioner's sugar; beat with an electric mixer until fluffy, about 1 minute. With a spoon, stir in the vanilla, flour, salt, and walnuts to form a stiff dough.

3. Using about 2 teaspoons of dough for each cookie, shape half the dough by rolling into balls between your hands. Place about 1½ inches apart on an ungreased baking sheet and bake about 12 minutes, until just pale golden on the bottom.

4. Meanwhile, sift ½ cup of the remaining confectioner's sugar into a 13-by-9-inch pan. As soon as the cookies are removed from the oven, use a spatula to transfer them to the sugar, tossing them around to coat; let the cookies cool completely in the sugar and then sift ¼ cup more sugar over them to coat.

5. Repeat with the remaining cookie dough, using a cool baking sheet to bake them and the remaining ¾ cup confectioner's sugar, divided as before, to coat.

DREAM FINGERS

These cookies are so light that they practically disintegrate
when you bite into them. To make them, the pecans must be sliced lengthwise
into paper-thin slivers with a sharp knife or they won't come out right.
It is a time-consuming chore, and one that can't be done by machine.

MAKES 3 DOZEN

1 cup (4 ounces) pecan halves
8 tablespoons (1 stick) unsalted
  butter, softened
1 cup plus 6 tablespoons sifted
  confectioner's sugar

1 cup all-purpose flour
1 ½ teaspoons water
1 teaspoon vanilla extract

1. Using a sharp knife, slice the pecans lengthwise into very thin slivers.

2. In a medium-sized bowl, using a handheld electric mixer, beat the butter with 2 tablespoons of the confectioner's sugar until fluffy, about 1 minute. With a spoon, stir in the flour, water, and vanilla to make a moderately stiff dough. Gently fold in the pecans until evenly distributed. Flatten the dough on waxed paper to a thickness of 1 inch; wrap and chill for about an hour, until firm. (Dough can be prepared a day or two ahead.)

3. Adjust a rack to the center of the oven and preheat to 250°F.

4. Using 2 level teaspoons of dough for each cookie, shape the dough into "cocoons" about 1 ½ inches long and ¾ inch wide. Place them on an ungreased baking sheet, leaving about 1 inch between them (all 3 dozen will fit onto one sheet as these do not spread). Bake for 1 hour, until barely beginning to turn pale golden.

5. Sift 1 cup of the remaining confectioner's sugar into a 13-by-9-inch pan. With a spatula, transfer the hot cookies to the sugar, carefully rolling them to coat with sugar. Let all of the cookies cool in the pan of sugar.

6. Sift 2 tablespoons of the remaining confectioner's sugar into a clean 13-by-9-inch pan. Arrange all of the cooled cookies over the sugar. Sift the remaining 2 tablespoons of sugar over the tops.

SHORTBREAD

The use of rendered chicken fat marks this
as a very old recipe. Although chicken fat was not an unusual ingredient in old
baking recipes, it is rarely called for today. The single tablespoon adds
dimension and flavor to these shortbread cookies.

MAKES 32 COOKIES

1 cup (2 sticks) unsalted butter,
   softened
1 tablespoon rendered chicken
   fat, chilled (see Note)

½ cup granulated sugar
2½ cups all-purpose flour

1. In a large bowl combine the butter, chicken fat, and sugar; beat with a handheld electric mixer until fluffy, 1 to 2 minutes. Add the flour and blend in with your fingers to make a stiff dough.

2. Divide the dough in half and place each piece on a square of waxed paper. Pat each into a 6-inch square, using a ruler or other straightedge to make the sides even. Top with a sheet of waxed paper and lightly draw the ruler over the paper to smooth the surface slightly. Refrigerate until firm, 3 hours or overnight.

3. Evenly space two racks in the oven and preheat to 300°F. Remove the squares of dough from the refrigerator and cut each into 16 equal 1½-inch squares. Place on ungreased baking sheets, leaving about 1 inch between squares. Bake until pale golden brown on the bottom, about 25 minutes, reversing the sheets halfway through the baking. Transfer to a rack with a spatula and cool completely.

Note: For rendered chicken fat, pull out any loose pieces of fat from the cavity of a chicken and pull off any pieces of fatty skin; finely chop fat and place in a small heavy saucepan or skillet along with about 2 tablespoons of water. Bring to a boil and then simmer until the water evaporates and the fat melts, about 10 minutes. Strain, cool, and chill. The rendered fat can be frozen for future use.

AUNT IRMA'S SUGAR COOKIES

Aunt Irma's secret in making these crisp sugar cookies
is in the kneading of the dough. As she finally explained to me, "You must knead
the dough by hand for at least fifteen minutes or the texture won't come out right."
Many tests proved her to be right. I am convinced that the warmth of your hands
as you knead contributes to the delicate texture.

MAKES ABOUT 5 DOZEN

3 cups all-purpose flour
1 teaspoon baking soda
1 teaspoon cream of tartar
¼ teaspoon salt
1½ cups granulated sugar

1 cup (2 sticks) unsalted butter,
    chilled and cut into thin slices
2 large eggs
1 teaspoon vanilla extract

ICING

1 cup sifted confectioner's sugar   2 tablespoons milk

1. In a medium-sized bowl, stir together the flour, baking soda, cream of tartar, and salt.

2. Place 1 cup of the granulated sugar in a large bowl and cut in the butter with a pastry blender until the mixture resembles coarse meal. Using a wooden spoon, beat in the eggs and vanilla. Add the dry ingredients and beat until blended.

3. Knead the dough by hand on a lightly floured surface, adding just enough flour to prevent the dough from sticking, for 15 minutes.

4. Preheat the oven to 350°F. Lightly grease two cookie sheets. Using your hands, roll the dough into walnut-size balls. Roll them in the remaining ½ cup granulated sugar to coat completely. Place 12 balls on each cookie sheet. Using the bottom of a glass dipped into granulated sugar, flatten each ball to about ¼-inch thickness. Bake until light brown, 12 to 15 minutes. Using a spatula, transfer the cookies to a rack.

5. Meanwhile, in a small bowl, stir together the confectioner's sugar and milk until smooth to make the icing. While the cookies are still hot, brush them with the icing to glaze. Repeat with the remaining cookie dough and icing. Let cool before serving.

FROSTED BUTTER COOKIES

This is the basic dough we used to make
fancy cookie-cutter cookies for the holidays. It produces a crisp, buttery cookie.
To decorate the cookies, you may want to divide the buttercream into thirds
and tint two of the batches different pale colors,
leaving the third batch uncolored.

MAKES ABOUT 5 DOZEN 2½-INCH COOKIES

1 cup (2 sticks) unsalted butter,
  softened
1 cup sifted confectioner's sugar

1 teaspoon vanilla extract
2¼ cups all-purpose flour

BUTTERCREAM

MAKES 1½ CUPS

8 tablespoons (1 stick) unsalted
  butter, softened
2½ cups sifted confectioner's sugar

4 teaspoons cold milk,
  approximately
½ teaspoon vanilla extract

1. In a medium-sized bowl, combine the butter, sugar, and vanilla; beat with a handheld electric mixer until fluffy, 1 to 2 minutes. With a spoon, stir in the flour to make a stiff dough. Divide the dough in half and place the two portions on separate sheets of waxed paper. Pat each piece of dough into a rectangle about 5 by 7 inches. Wrap in waxed paper and chill for 1 hour or overnight.

2. Evenly space two racks in the oven and preheat to 375°F. Let the dough soften for about 10 minutes before rolling.

3. Place one piece of the dough between sheets of waxed paper and roll it about ⅛ inch thick; it will be a rectangle measuring approximately 8 by 14 inches. Using decorative cookie cutters about 2½ inches in diameter, cut out as many cookies as possible; with a spatula, space them at least ½ inch apart on a cool ungreased baking sheet. Refrigerate the scraps. Repeat with the second piece of dough, using a second baking sheet. Bake 10 to 14 minutes, until light golden brown. If the cookies are browning unevenly, turn the sheets or reverse their positions halfway through baking. Reroll the scraps of dough, making as many cookies as possible. With a spatula, transfer the cookies to a rack and cool completely before frosting.

4. While the cookies are cooling, prepare the buttercream. In a medium-sized bowl, with a handheld electric mixer, beat the butter until fluffy, about 1 minute. Gradually beat in half of the sifted sugar. Beat in the rest alternately with half-teaspoonfuls of the milk and the vanilla to make a frosting with a good spreading consistency, beating in a few drops more milk if necessary. Cover if not using right away. (If refrigerated, the buttercream will set. It is best to use this as soon as possible after making it.)

5. Divide the buttercream into three equal portions and tint two of them a pale color with about a half drop of food coloring, or less. The color will look best if pale. Leave one uncolored. With a spatula, spread the cookies with the two tinted buttercreams. Fit a pastry bag with a small plain round tip and fill it with the uncolored buttercream. Pipe designs and borders onto the frosted cookies as desired. Leave on racks until the buttercream sets, about 1 hour.

FINNISH COOKIES

These cookies are so rich and flaky,
they seem almost like almond-flavored pastry. The dough is spread with beaten egg white, then sprinkled with sugar and finely chopped walnuts.

MAKES ABOUT 4 DOZEN

1 cup (2 sticks) unsalted butter, softened	½ teaspoon almond extract
½ cup granulated sugar	Pinch of salt
1 large egg, separated	½ cup (2 ounces) finely chopped walnuts
2 cups all-purpose flour	

1. In a large bowl combine the butter, ¼ cup of the sugar and the egg yolk; with a handheld electric mixer, beat until light and fluffy, 1 to 2 minutes. With a spoon, stir in the flour and almond extract to make a stiff dough. Divide the dough into two equal pieces and shape them into 6-inch squares on separate sheets of waxed paper. Wrap and chill thoroughly (at least 1 hour or as long as a day or two). Let the dough soften at room temperature about 15 minutes before rolling.

2. Evenly space two racks in the oven and preheat to 350°F.

3. On a lightly floured board, roll one piece of the dough out to a 10-inch square about ⅛ inch thick. This dough is very short and breaks easily; simply pinch any tears together, flour the surface, and continue rolling. Chill the rolled dough on the board. Using a second board and the second piece of dough, roll and chill as before.

4. Place the egg white in a small bowl and add a pinch of salt. With a handheld electric mixer or a whisk, beat the white to a stage between foamy and in soft peaks. Have the remaining ¼ cup of sugar and the walnuts within arm's reach. Quickly spread the beaten egg white over each square of dough. Sprinkle each square evenly with 2 tablespoons of the sugar and ¼ cup of the walnuts. With a pastry cutter or sharp knife, cut into 24 pieces by cutting horizontally into equal thirds and then vertically into eight equal widths (the pieces will be approximately 1 by 3 inches). Transfer with a spatula to an ungreased baking sheet. Bake 15 to 20 minutes, until light golden brown. Transfer to a rack and cool.

5. Repeat the procedure with the remaining square of dough.

AUNT IRMA'S SOUR CREAM TWISTS

One of Aunt Irma's all-time favorite recipes.
These flaky yeast-based cookies are flavored with sour cream and coated with sugar.
The light sweetness comes from the sugar coating, as there is
only one teaspoon of sugar in the dough.

MAKES ABOUT 10 DOZEN

3 tablespoons warm water (105° to 115°F)
1 cup granulated sugar
One ¼-ounce package active dry yeast
3¾ cups all-purpose flour
1 teaspoon salt

8 tablespoons (1 stick) unsalted butter, sliced
½ cup vegetable shortening
2 egg yolks, lightly beaten
1 cup sour cream, at room temperature
1 teaspoon vanilla extract

1. Combine the water with 1 teaspoon of the sugar in a small bowl. Sprinkle the yeast over the water and let it soften for a minute or two. Stir to dissolve the yeast and let proof until foamy, about 5 minutes.

2. In a large bowl, combine the flour and salt. Cut in the butter and shortening with a pastry blender until the mixture resembles coarse meal. Stir down the proofed yeast and add it along with the egg yolks, sour cream, and vanilla. Stir with a wooden spoon until well blended. Cover the bowl and let rest in a cool place (about 60°F) for 2 hours.

3. Evenly space two oven racks and preheat the oven to 375°F. Lightly grease two baking sheets. Divide the dough in half and reserve one half, covered, until needed. Reserve ½ cup of the sugar and place the remaining sugar on a small plate. Sprinkle your work surface with about 1 tablespoon of the sugar on the plate. Place the dough on the work surface and pat it into a rectangle about 4 by 5 inches; sprinkle with about 1 tablespoon of sugar and roll dough out thinner with a rolling pin, turning it several times and sprinkling the top with about 2 teaspoons sugar at a time, until the dough measures 13 by 17 inches and is about ⅛ inch thick, or slightly thicker. Sprinkle the top with about 1 tablespoon sugar and trim the rectangle to measure 12 by 16 inches.

4. Using a ruler and a pastry wheel with a crimped edge or a sharp knife, cut the dough into strips 4 inches long and ¾ inch wide. One at a time, pick up the strips, dip the bottom surface into the sugar remaining on the plate, turn one end over so that the dough twists in the middle, and place on a baking sheet about ½ inch apart.

5. Bake until crisp and golden brown, about 15 mintues. Transfer to racks to cool. Repeat with the remaining dough and remaining ½ cup sugar.

SPRINGERLE

Another of our favorite Christmas cookies.
My mother's original recipe calls for a dozen eggs and three pounds of confectioner's sugar. She'd roll them out to cover the entire table top, then leave them overnight to air-dry before baking them.

MAKES 6 TO 8 DOZEN 1-BY-1½-INCH COOKIES

4 large eggs
3½ cups confectioner's sugar
½ teaspoon anise extract
   or oil
3½ cups all-purpose flour

1 teaspoon baker's ammonia
   (ammonium hydrogen
   carbonate or *Hirschhorn-Salz*);
   see Note
1 teaspoon baking powder

1. In a large mixing bowl, beat the eggs with an electric mixer at medium-high speed for 30 minutes, until a thick ribbon is formed when the beaters are lifted. Gradually beat in the sugar and then beat in the anise extract.

2. In a medium-sized bowl combine the flour, baker's ammonia, and baking powder; stir together to blend. Beat 1 cup of the flour mixture into the eggs and sugar. Beat in about 1 cup more, and then, with a spoon, stir in the remaining flour to make a soft dough that is just slightly sticky.

3. On a generously floured surface, roll out half the dough to a rectangle that measures approximately 10 by 12 inches (it will be slightly less than ¼ inch thick). If using a springerle rolling pin, roll over the dough once to leave clear impressions on the dough; if using a springerle mold, press onto dough to leave impression. With a pastry wheel or knife, cut the cookies. Lightly sprinkle a work surface or trays with flour and transfer the cookies to the surface. Let air-dry overnight to set designs.

4. Position an oven rack in the center of the oven and preheat to 300°F. Lightly grease a baking sheet. With a spatula, transfer enough springerle to the sheet to fill it, leaving 1 inch between them. Bake 15 to 20 minutes, until they just begin to turn color; do not let them brown. Transfer to a rack and cool completely. Store in airtight containers. Springerle keep for many weeks, in fact, some suggest letting them stand in a cookie jar or tin for at least two weeks before eating.

Note: Baker's ammonia is a preservative with a drying quality. It is used in springerle to make the cookies white, light, and hard. My mother always bought it in crystal rock form and shaved it with a paring knife to make a powder. I have found it only in baking-supply stores in little envelopes of powder.

AUNT MYRA'S FUDGE BROWNIES

Dense and fudgy, these brownies have been family favorites for more than three decades. Sometimes the top is covered with fudge frosting and sometimes not. Either way, they are always a hit.

MAKES 16 SMALL SQUARES

8 tablespoons (1 stick) unsalted butter
4 ounces (4 squares) semisweet chocolate, coarsely chopped
2 large eggs, at room temperature
Pinch of salt

⅔ cup granulated sugar
2 teaspoons vanilla extract
½ cup all-purpose flour
1 cup (4 ounces) coarsely chopped walnuts (optional)

FUDGE FROSTING

MAKES ¾ CUP

¼ cup heavy cream
4 ounces semisweet chocolate, coarsely chopped

¼ cup sifted confectioner's sugar

1. Position a rack in the center of the oven and preheat to 325°F. Line an 8-inch square pan with aluminum foil and lightly butter the foil.

2. In a small saucepan over low heat, melt the butter. Remove from the heat and add the chocolate. Let stand for 5 minutes and then stir until smooth.

3. In a large bowl combine the eggs and salt; beat with a handheld electric mixer until frothy, about 30 seconds. Gradually beat in the sugar and continue to beat until light, 1 t\ 2 minutes. Add the vanilla and the melted chocolate and butter, beating until smooth. With a spoon, stir in the flour just until blended. Stir in the walnuts if you wish to use them and turn the batter into the prepared pan. Bake for about 30 minutes, until a toothpick inserted near the center emerges with a few crumbs clinging to it. Do not overbake or the brownies will be dry. Place the pan on a rack and cool to room temperature.

4. While the brownies are cooling, prepare the frosting, which is optional but a delicious addition. In a small heavy saucepan over very low heat, combine the cream and chocolate. Stirring constantly, heat just until melted and smooth. Remove from heat and stir in the confectioner's sugar.

5. With a knife, loosen the edge all around and pull out the cooled brownies by the aluminum foil and invert on a board. Peel off and discard foil. Return the brownies to the pan right side up and spread with fudge frosting. Let stand in a cool place for an hour or two. Cut into 16 small squares with a sharp knife.

BLONDIES

First cousin to the brownie, these moist and chewy squares
are made without chocolate. Because they travel well, they are a good choice for
school lunchboxes or outings of any kind.

MAKES 16 SMALL SQUARES

8 tablespoons (1 stick) unsalted
   butter, softened
1 cup packed light brown sugar
1 large egg
1½ teaspoons vanilla extract
1 cup all-purpose flour

½ teaspoon baking powder
¼ teaspoon baking soda
Pinch of salt
1 cup (4 ounces) coarsely
   chopped pecans

1. Adjust a rack to the center of the oven and preheat to 350°F. Line an 8-inch square pan with aluminum foil and lightly butter the foil.

2. In a large bowl, using a handheld electric mixer, beat the butter until fluffy, about 1 minute. Add the brown sugar, egg, and vanilla; beat until thick and light, 1 to 2 minutes.

3. On a sheet of waxed paper, stir together the flour, baking powder, baking soda, and salt. With a spoon, quickly stir the dry ingredients into the butter mixture. Stir in the pecans. Turn the batter into the prepared pan. Bake for about 30 minutes, until a toothpick inserted near the center emerges with a few crumbs clinging to it. Place the pan on a rack and cool to room temperature. With a knife, loosen the edge all around and pull out the blondies by the aluminum foil and invert on a board. Peel off and discard the foil. Turn the blondies right side up and cut into 16 small squares.

LEMON BARS

After many trials with various recipes for lemon bars from the family files,
I finally found one that called for beating the mixture for ten minutes to thicken it.
This allowed me to cut down a bit on the amount of sugar and to add extra lemon
juice to produce these still sweet, intensely lemon-flavored bars.

MAKES 12

1 cup plus 2 tablespoons
  all-purpose flour
¼ cup plus 1 tablespoon
  confectioner's sugar
8 tablespoons (1 stick) cold
  unsalted butter, sliced

2 large eggs
¾ cup granulated sugar
½ teaspoon grated lemon zest
¼ cup fresh lemon juice
¼ teaspoon baking powder
Pinch of salt

1. Position a rack in the center of the oven and preheat to 350°F. In a medium-sized bowl stir together 1 cup of the flour and ¼ cup of the confectioner's sugar. Cut in the butter until it resembles coarse meal and then work it with your fingertips until dough holds together. Press evenly into the bottom of an ungreased 8-inch square pan. Bake about 15 minutes, until light golden brown. Remove, but leave the oven on.

2. Meanwhile, in a medium-sized bowl, with an electric mixer, beat the eggs until frothy. Gradually beat in the granulated sugar. Add the lemon zest and lemon juice; beat at high speed for 10 minutes, until smooth and slightly thickened.

3. On a sheet of waxed paper combine the remaining 2 tablespoons flour with the baking powder and salt; gradually beat into the egg mixture, beating just until smooth. Pour over the baked layer and bake about 20 minutes longer, until set and lightly browned. Cool in the pan on a rack. Sift the remaining 1 tablespoon confectioner's sugar over the top and cut into 12 bars.

CHEWY CHEWS

I was happily surprised to find that this old recipe contains no butter.
The richness and moisture of the bars derives from the chopped dates and eggs.
The finished squares are rolled in granulated sugar
for a pleasing change in texture.

MAKES 36

¾ cup sifted cake flour
¾ teaspoon baking powder
¼ teaspoon salt
¾ cup packed light brown sugar
1 cup (6 ounces) chopped pitted
   dates

1 cup (4 ounces) chopped
   walnuts
2 large eggs, lightly beaten
¼ cup granulated sugar, for
   coating

1. Adjust a rack to the center of the oven and preheat to 350°F. Line an 8-inch square pan with aluminum foil and lightly butter the foil.

2. In a medium-sized bowl stir together the cake flour, baking powder, salt, and sugar. Stir in the dates and walnuts. Add the beaten eggs and stir just to moisten. Spread into the prepared pan. Bake 30 to 35 minutes, until the top springs back when very lightly touched. Cool in the pan on a rack for 15 minutes.

3. While still warm, run a knife around the pan to loosen the pan of chewy chews. Invert a board over the top and then invert both to unmold. Peel off the aluminum foil. With a sharp heavy knife, cut into 36 equal squares. Place the ¼ cup granulated sugar on a dinner plate and roll the cubes of chewy chews in it to coat lightly. Let cool to room temperature before serving.

CHOCOLATE CHIP BARS

If you are short of time these quick and easy-to-make bars
are a good alternative to chocolate chip cookies. And unlike the more fragile cookies,
they are easily wrapped individually and packaged for bake sales,
brown bag lunches, and picnics.

MAKES 24

1¼ cups all-purpose flour
½ teaspoon baking soda
½ teaspoon salt
8 tablespoons (1 stick) unsalted
   butter, softened
½ cup packed light brown sugar
⅓ cup granulated sugar

1 large egg
1½ teaspoons vanilla extract
½ cup (2 ounces) chopped
   walnuts
One 6-ounce package semisweet
   chocolate chips

1. Position a rack in the center of the oven and preheat to 375°F. Butter and flour an 11¾-by-7½-inch pan.

2. In a medium-sized bowl stir together the flour, baking soda, and salt. In a large mixing bowl combine the butter, brown sugar, and granulated sugar. With a hand-held electric mixer beat until fluffy, 1 to 2 minutes. With a spoon, stir in the dry ingredients to make a stiff batter. Stir in the walnuts and chocolate chips. Spread evenly in the prepared pan. Bake until golden brown (a toothpick inserted 2 inches in from the side of the pan will emerge with a few crumbs clinging to it), 20 to 25 minutes. Place the pan on a rack and cool to room temperature. Cut lengthwise down the center and then make 11 crosswise cuts to produce 24 thin bars.

APPLE BARS

Dense country-style apple bars
are fortified with oats and walnuts and spiced with
cinnamon, cloves, and nutmeg.

MAKES 24

12 tablespoons (1½ sticks)
   unsalted butter, softened
1 cup packed dark brown sugar
2 large eggs
1¼ cups all-purpose flour
1 teaspoon baking powder
½ teaspooon baking soda
½ teaspoon salt
1 teaspoon ground cinnamon
½ teaspoon grated nutmeg

¼ teaspoon ground cloves
1 cup old-fashioned rolled oats
1 cup (4 ounces) chopped
   walnuts
2 large (6 to 8 ounces each) tart
   green cooking apples, peeled,
   cored, and cut into ¼-inch dice
   (about 2 cups)
2 tablespoons sifted confectioner's
   sugar, for topping

1. Position a rack in the center of the oven and preheat to 375°F. Butter a 13-by-9-inch pan.

2. In a large bowl combine the butter and brown sugar. With a handheld electric mixer beat until fluffy. Beat in the eggs one at a time.

3. In a medium-sized bowl, stir together the flour, baking powder, baking soda, salt, cinnamon, nutmeg, and cloves. Stir the dry ingredients into the butter-sugar mixture just to blend. Stir in the oats, walnuts, and apples and turn into the prepared pan. Spread evenly and bake 25 to 30 minutes, until the top springs back when lightly touched. Place on a rack and cool to room temperature. Sift the confectioner's sugar over the top. Cut in thirds lengthwise and eighths crosswise to make 24 bars.

RASPBERRY-PECAN BARS

Raspberry lovers will be pleased with this recipe
for really good cookielike bars sandwiched with raspberry preserves. You may also
use apricot jam as a filling; it is equally delicious.

MAKES 20

2 cups all-purpose flour
1 teaspoon baking powder
¼ teaspoon baking soda
¼ teaspoon salt
12 tablespoons (1½ sticks)
   unsalted butter, softened
¼ cup granulated sugar

½ cup packed light brown sugar
2 egg yolks
1 teaspoon vanilla extract
1 cup (4 ounces) chopped pecans
⅔ cup raspberry jam
2 tablespoons fresh lemon juice

1. Position a rack in the center of the oven and preheat to 325°F. Butter an 11¾-by-7½-inch baking pan.

2. In a medium-sized bowl, stir together the flour, baking powder, baking soda, and salt. In a large mixing bowl, with a handheld electric mixer, beat the butter until creamy, about 1 minute. Gradually add the sugars and continue to beat until light and fluffy, 1 to 2 minutes. Beat in the egg yolks and vanilla. With a spoon, stir in the dry ingredients. Reserve 3 tablespoons of the pecans and stir in the remainder.

3. In a small bowl, stir together the jam and the lemon juice.

4. Press about half of the dough evenly in the bottom of the pan. Spread with the flavored jam. Crumble the rest of the dough evenly over the top (it is sticky so this is a bit of work but use floured hands and persist). Sprinkle with the reserved 3 tablespoons pecans. Bake 50 to 60 minutes, until golden brown and firm. Cool in the pan on a rack. Cut lengthwise down the center and then crosswise into 10 even widths to make 20 bars.

DATE CRUMBLE BARS

This very old recipe of Grandmother Wahlstrom's
has been baked for at least three generations of children in our family. The bars
may be served just slightly warm, if you wish. Because they hold up well,
they are a very good choice for packing into lunchboxes.

MAKES 24

DATE FILLING

10 ounces pitted dates (35 to 40), halved
2 tablespoons granulated sugar

1 cup water
2 tablespoons fresh lemon juice

CRUMB CRUST AND TOPPING

2½ cups old-fashioned rolled oats
1½ cups all-purpose flour
¾ cup packed light brown sugar
½ teaspoon baking soda

Pinch of salt
1 cup (2 sticks) unsalted butter, softened

1. Prepare the date filling: In a heavy medium-sized saucepan, combine the dates and sugar with 1 cup of water. Bring to a boil over moderate heat. Reduce the heat to low and simmer, stirring frequently, until thick and jamlike, about 20 minutes. Remove from the heat and stir in the lemon juice. Cool to room temperature.

2. Adjust a rack to the center of the oven and preheat to 350°F. Lightly butter a 13-by-9-inch pan.

3. Prepare the crumb crust and topping: In a large bowl stir together the oats, flour, brown sugar, baking soda, and salt. Add the butter and crumble with your fingers until blended. Pat half of the mixture into the bottom of the baking pan and spread all of the date filling evenly over it. Crumble the rest of the oat mixture over the top, patting lightly. Bake 25 to 30 minutes, until golden brown. Cool on a rack to room temperature. Cut into 24 bars.

APRICOT BARS

Plumped-up dried apricots add flavor and moisture
to the filling baked over a short pastry for these rich bars. After they have been
cooled, the finished bars are rolled in confectioner's sugar.

MAKES 24

BOTTOM LAYER

1 cup all-purpose flour
¼ cup granulated sugar

8 tablespoons (1 stick) unsalted
 butter, softened

TOP LAYER

½ cup packed (4 ounces) ½-inch
 pieces dried apricots
2 large eggs
¾ cup packed light brown sugar
1 teaspoon vanilla extract
⅓ cup all-purpose flour

½ teaspoon baking powder
¼ teaspoon salt
½ cup (2 ounces) chopped
 walnuts
½ cup sifted confectioner's sugar,
 for coating

1. Position a rack in the center of the oven and preheat to 350°F. Butter an 11¾-by-7½-inch baking pan.

2. Prepare the bottom layer: In a medium-sized bowl combine the flour and sugar; with a spoon, work in the butter to make a sticky dough. Spread in the prepared pan in an even layer. Bake 20 to 25 minutes, until golden brown. Remove, but leave oven on.

3. Meanwhile, prepare the top layer: In a small heavy saucepan combine the apricots with ¾ cup water. Place over moderate heat and bring to a boil. Simmer until tender, 10 to 15 minutes. Drain and let cool for a few minutes.

4. In a large bowl combine the eggs and brown sugar. With a handheld electric mixer, beat until light, 1 to 2 minutes. Beat in the vanilla. On a sheet of waxed paper, stir together the flour, baking powder, and salt; add to the egg mixture and stir with a spoon, just to blend. Stir in the drained apricots and the walnuts. Spread over the bottom layer (it can be hot, fresh from the oven) and bake 30 to 35 minutes, until lightly browned; the top will spring back when lightly touched and a toothpick

inserted in the center will emerge clean. Place on a rack and cool to room temperature. Cut crosswise into equal fourths and lengthwise into equal sixths, making 24 bars.

5. Place the confectioner's sugar on a plate and roll the bars in it just to coat on all sides.

CHERRY WALNUT BARS

The candied cherries for these moist and chewy bars
are put to soak in two teaspoons of vanilla, intensifying their flavor. Combined with
the walnuts in the batter, they create a dense, fruitcakelike bar.

MAKES 12

BOTTOM LAYER

1 cup all-purpose flour
8 tablespoons (1 stick) unsalted butter, softened

3 tablespoons confectioner's sugar

TOP LAYER

¾ cup (6 ounces) halved candied red cherries
2 teaspoons vanilla extract
2 large eggs
⅔ cup granulated sugar

¼ cup all-purpose flour
½ teaspoon baking powder
¼ teaspoon salt
¾ cup (3 ounces) chopped walnuts

1. Position a rack in the center of the oven and preheat to 350°F. Butter an 8-inch square pan.

2. Prepare the bottom layer: In a medium-sized bowl combine the flour, butter, and confectioner's sugar; beat together until smooth. Turn into the prepared pan and pat even with your fingers. Bake until golden brown, about 25 minutes. When you remove the pan, leave the oven on.

3. Meanwhile, prepare the top layer: In a small bowl, combine the candied cherries with the vanilla; toss together and let stand until needed. In a large bowl with a handheld electric mixer, beat the eggs slightly. Gradually beat in the sugar and beat until thick and light, 1 to 2 minutes. On a sheet of waxed paper, stir together the flour, baking powder, and salt. With a spoon, stir the dry ingredients into the egg mixture just until well blended. Stir in the walnuts and vanilla-macerated cherries. When the bottom layer emerges from the oven, spread the top layer evenly over it and bake about 25 minutes longer, until deep golden brown. When done the top will spring back when very lightly touched. Cool in the pan on a rack. Cut in half in one direction and then into 6 sections in the opposite direction.

Coconut Bars

These delectable bars consist of a rich coconut macaroonlike filling flecked with slivered almonds baked over a golden crust.

MAKES 12

BOTTOM LAYER

8 tablespoons (1 stick) unsalted butter, softened

1 cup all-purpose flour
1 tablespoon packed light brown sugar

TOP LAYER

2 large eggs
1 teaspoon vanilla extract
¾ cup packed light brown sugar
1 tablespoon all-purpose flour
½ teaspoon baking powder
⅛ teaspoon ground cinnamon

1 cup (4 ounces) slivered almonds
½ cup (about 1½ ounces) lightly packed sweetened shredded coconut

1. Adjust a rack to the middle of the oven and preheat to 325°F. Lightly butter an 8-inch square pan.

2. Prepare the bottom layer: In a medium-sized bowl, combine the butter, flour, and brown sugar and mix well with a spoon. Turn the dough into the prepared pan and spread it evenly. Bake until light golden brown, about 20 minutes. Remove, but leave the oven on.

3. Meanwhile, prepare the top layer: In a medium-sized bowl, using a handheld electric mixer, beat the eggs, vanilla, and brown sugar until light, 1 to 2 minutes. With a spoon, stir in the flour, baking powder, cinnamon, almonds, and coconut until blended. As soon as the bottom layer is removed from the oven, spread the top layer evenly over it and return to the oven and bake for about 30 minutes longer, until golden brown. Cool to room temperature in the pan on a rack. With a sharp knife, cut into 12 bars.

WALNUT SQUARES

Rich ground walnuts flavored with cinnamon and brown sugar
form a moist and chewy topping for a layer of short, sweet pastry. Cut into
little squares, they make a perfect treat with coffee, tea, or milk.

MAKES 16

8 tablespoons (1 stick) unsalted
   butter, softened
⅔ cup packed dark brown sugar
1 teaspoon vanilla extract
¼ teaspoon salt

1 large egg, separated
1¼ cups all-purpose flour
1 cup (4 ounces) chopped
   walnuts
½ teaspoon ground cinnamon

1. Position a rack in the center of the oven and preheat to 375°F. Lightly butter a 9-inch square pan.

2. Prepare the bottom layer: In a medium-sized bowl combine the butter with ⅓ cup of the brown sugar. With a handheld electric mixer, beat until fluffy, about 1 minute. Add the vanilla, salt, and the egg yolk; beat until thick and light, 1 to 2 minutes. With a spoon, stir in the flour. With floured fingertips, press evenly into the prepared pan. Bake 10 to 12 minutes, until light golden brown around the edges. Remove, but leave the oven on.

3. Meanwhile, prepare the top layer: In a medium-sized bowl, with a handheld electric mixer, beat the egg white until frothy. Add the remaining ⅓ cup brown sugar and beat until smooth and glossy, 2 to 3 minutes. Fold in the walnuts and cinnamon. As soon as the bottom layer emerges from the oven, spread with the walnut topping. Return to the oven and bake about 15 minutes, until the top is golden brown and firm to the touch. Cool in the pan on a rack for 20 to 30 minutes. Cut into 16 squares while warm, and then cool to room temperature.

Norwegian Almond Bars

The latticelike strips of sweet pastry dough
arranged over the rich almond filling make these bars as decorative as they are
delicious. Although the pastry is a little difficult to work with, it doesn't matter
if some of the strips for the lattice topping break. Just put them in place
atop the filling, brush with the glaze, and they'll bake up fine.

MAKES 24

SWEET PASTRY

2 cups all-purpose flour
2 teaspoons baking powder
½ cup granulated sugar

1 cup (2 sticks) chilled unsalted
  butter, thinly sliced
1 large egg, lightly beaten

ALMOND FILLING

1½ cups (7½ ounces) blanched
  slivered almonds, ground
1½ cups sifted confectioner's
  sugar

1 egg white (reserve yolk for
  glaze)
¼ teaspoon almond extract
2 tablespoons water

GLAZE

1 egg yolk

1 teaspoon water

1. Prepare the sweet pastry: In a large bowl combine the flour, baking powder, and sugar; cut in the butter with a pastry blender until the mixture resembles coarse meal. Add the egg and stir with a fork until the dough holds together. Cut off two-thirds of the dough and press it into an ungreased 13-by-9-inch pan to make an even layer. Refrigerate. Place the remaining third of the dough on a sheet of waxed paper and top with another sheet of waxed paper. Pat the dough into a 5-by-10-inch rectangle and refrigerate until firm.

2. Position a rack in the center of the oven and preheat to 350°F.

3. Prepare the almond filling: In a food processor combine almonds, confectioner's sugar, egg white, almond extract, and water; grind to a coarse paste. Without a food processor, grind the almonds and stir them into the remaining filling ingredients.

Remove the pastry-lined pan from the refrigerator and spread all of the almond filling over it.

4. Cut the 5-by-10-inch piece of pastry lengthwise into strips about ¾ inch wide. Using a small spatula, carefully lift up the strips, one at a time, and place them on the diagonal, in a lattice pattern, over the top of the filling, trimming them to fit as needed. It will not matter if the fragile strips break; simply piece them together as you arrange them.

5. Stir together the egg yolk and 1 teaspoon water and brush some of this glaze over the strips of pastry. Bake 35 to 40 minutes, until the top is golden and the sides begin to pull away from the pan. Cool in the pan on a rack. To make 24 bars, cut crosswise into 4 equal pieces and then lengthwise into 6 equal widths.

PECAN FINGERS

The pastry layer for these rich bars is topped
with brown sugar and pecans. When they emerge from the oven, an orange icing
is melted atop the layer of pecans to create an unexpected zesty taste.

MAKES 24

BOTTOM LAYER

8 tablespoons (1 stick) unsalted
   butter, softened
¼ cup vegetable shortening

½ cup sifted confectioner's sugar
1½ cups all-purpose flour

TOP LAYER

2 large eggs
¾ cup packed dark brown sugar
2 tablespoons all-purpose flour

½ teaspoon baking powder
1 teaspoon vanilla extract
1 cup (4 ounces) chopped pecans

ORANGE ICING

1 cup sifted confectioner's sugar
2 tablespoons melted butter
1 teaspoon grated orange zest

3 tablespoons fresh orange juice
1 tablespoon fresh lemon juice

1. Position a rack in the center of the oven and preheat to 350°F.

2. Prepare the bottom layer: In a medium-sized bowl, with a handheld electric mixer, beat the butter, shortening, and confectioner's sugar together until fluffy. With a spoon, stir in the flour. Press evenly in the bottom of an ungreased 13-by-9-inch baking pan. Bake until lightly browned, 12 to 15 minutes. Remove, but leave the oven on.

3. Meanwhile, prepare the top layer: In a medium-sized bowl combine the eggs and brown sugar and beat until light, 1 to 2 minutes. With a spoon, stir in the flour, baking powder, vanilla, and pecans until evenly blended. Spoon over the bottom layer as soon as it emerges from the oven, spreading the top layer evenly. Bake until golden brown, about 20 minutes.

4. While the top layer is baking, prepare the orange icing: In a small bowl combine the confectioner's sugar, melted butter, orange zest, orange juice, and lemon juice; stir until smooth.

5. Let the pan of bars cool on a rack for 10 minutes and then spread with the orange icing. Cool to room temperature and then cut into 24 bars, cutting crosswise in 4 even sections and lengthwise in 6 equal portions.

CHOCOLATE-PEANUT SQUARES

Chunky with peanuts and chocolate,
these old-fashioned frosted bars are a great favorite with children and with anyone else who, like me, is partial to these ingredients.

MAKES 16

BOTTOM LAYER

1 cup (about 5 ounces) chopped
   unsalted roasted peanuts
½ cup all-purpose flour
½ cup packed light brown sugar

¼ teaspoon baking soda
¼ teaspoon salt
5 tablespoons unsalted butter,
   melted

TOP LAYER

3 tablespoons unsalted butter
2 ounces (2 squares)
   unsweetened chocolate,
   chopped
1 large egg

¾ cup granulated sugar
⅔ cup all-purpose flour
¼ teaspoon salt
¼ cup milk
1 teaspoon vanilla extract

FROSTING

¼ cup heavy cream
4 ounces (4 squares) semisweet
   chocolate, chopped

1. Position a rack in the center of the oven and preheat to 350°F. Butter an 8-inch square pan.

2. Prepare the bottom layer: In a medium-size bowl combine the peanuts, flour, brown sugar, baking soda, and salt. Stir in the melted butter until blended. Turn into the baking pan and lightly pat into an even layer.

3. Prepare the top layer: In a small heavy saucepan combine the butter and chocolate. Place over low heat and stir just until smooth. Remove from the heat.

4. In a medium-sized bowl, with a handheld electric mixer, beat the egg with the sugar until light, 1 to 2 minutes. Beat in the chocolate mixture. On a sheet of waxed paper, stir together the flour and salt. Stir the dry ingredients into the chocolate mixture alternately with the milk, beginning and ending with flour. Stir in the vanilla. Spread evenly over the peanut layer and bake for 30 to 35 minutes, until the top springs back when very lightly touched. Cool on a rack for 10 minutes.

5. Meanwhile, prepare the frosting: Place the heavy cream in a small heavy saucepan over low heat. When it comes to a bare simmer, remove from the heat and stir in the chocolate until smooth. Spread over the chocolate layer while slightly warm. Cool thoroughly and cut into 16 squares.

CHEESECAKE SQUARES

Aunt Irma was partial to cheesecake and
anything resembling it. More often than not, she included these rich little squares
in the assortment of cookies set out for visits by her nieces and nephews.

MAKES 16

BOTTOM LAYER

6 tablespoons (¾ stick) unsalted
 butter, softened
⅓ cup packed light brown sugar

1 cup all-purpose flour
½ cup (2 ounces) finely chopped
 walnuts

TOP LAYER

One 8-ounce package cream
 cheese, softened
¼ cup granulated sugar
1 large egg
2 tablespoons milk

1 teaspoon vanilla extract
½ teaspoon grated lemon zest
1 tablespoon fresh lemon juice
2 tablespoons (½ ounce) finely
 chopped walnuts

1. Position a rack in the center of the oven and preheat to 350°F. Butter an 8-inch square pan.

2. Prepare the bottom layer: In a medium-sized mixing bowl, with a handheld electric mixer, beat the butter and brown sugar together until light and fluffy, 1 to 2 minutes. With a spoon, stir in the flour and walnuts to make a stiff dough. Remove ¾ cup of the dough for the topping and press the remaining ¾ cup into the prepared pan in an even layer. Bake 12 to 15 minutes, until golden brown. Remove, but leave the oven on.

3. Meanwhile, prepare the top layer: In a medium-sized bowl with a handheld electric mixer, beat the cream cheese and sugar together until smooth. Beat in the egg, milk, and vanilla until blended and then beat in the lemon zest and lemon juice. Spread the filling over the bottom layer. Crumble the reserved ¾ cup of dough over the top and sprinkle with 2 tablespoons walnuts. Bake about 25 minutes, until golden brown around the edges. Place on a rack and cool to room temperature. Cut into 16 small squares. To store, wrap in plastic wrap and refrigerate.

OLD-FASHIONED
❧ DESSERTS ❧

These old-fashioned desserts are simple American fare at its freshest and best. Many have a history that can be traced back to various groups of early settlers in this country; and like much cookery dating back over a long period of time, many are associated with particular seasons of the year. Some of the recipes—cream puffs, éclairs, cream horns—do not belong to any special time of year. But I consider rice pudding and buttered bread pudding to be among the greatest comforts of winter, while strawberry shortcake joyously signals the arrival of spring. Desserts made with peaches, raspberries, and blueberries still evoke for me the sensuous fullness of summer, and the image of my mother removing the peel of an apple in a continuous spiral strip to make a favorite apple dessert is an unmistakable sign of the approach of autumn.

These traditional favorites were among the recipes most assiduously tested and traded by my mother and my four aunts, so that the ones offered in this book represent the best of many versions. It was agreed that Aunt Charlotte made the best apple crisp, so it is her recipe that is given here. When apple pudding was required, we always used my grandmother's recipe, and my grandmother's gingerbread recipe was also the general family favorite, most often served with mounds of freshly whipped cream. On the rare occasions when some portion of dessert was left over, we would have it for breakfast the next morning.

Whatever your fancy, you can rely on these desserts to be familiar and comforting and every bit as good as you remember. Many can be put into the oven just before you sit down to dinner, so that by the time you feel ready for dessert they are at exactly the right temperature. But whether you serve them warm or cold, plain or accompanied by a little heavy cream or whipped cream, these desserts are guaranteed to be nothing less than completely satisfying.

STRAWBERRY SHORTCAKE

This was an extra-special favorite in our household.

MAKES 6 SERVINGS

3 pints ripe strawberries

6 to 8 tablespoons granulated sugar

SHORTCAKES

2 cups all-purpose flour
2 tablespoons granulated sugar
1 tablespoon baking powder
¼ teaspoon salt

4 tablespoons (½ stick) chilled
   unsalted butter, thinly sliced
¼ cup vegetable shortening
½ cup milk

TOPPING

½ cup heavy cream
1 tablespoon granulated sugar

½ teaspoon vanilla extract

1. Quickly rinse the berries in cold water, hull them and set two-thirds of the best strawberries aside. Cut the remaining one-third into quarters and place them in a large bowl. Stir in 6 tablespoons of the sugar and lightly mash the berries with a potato masher or a fork. Add the whole berries, cover, and refrigerate until chilled, at least one hour, stirring once or twice. Taste for sweetness and add 1 or 2 tablespoons more sugar if desired; stir to dissolve.

2. Adjust an oven rack to the center of the oven; preheat to 400°F.

3. In a large mixing bowl, combine the flour, sugar, baking powder, and salt. Using a pastry blender or two knives, cut in the butter and shortening until the mixture resembles coarse meal. Drizzle half of the milk over the top and stir quickly, just to moisten. Drizzle the remaining milk over the mixture and stir just to blend evenly. The dough should be moist enough to hold together when pressed.

4. Turn the dough out onto a lightly floured surface and gently knead for 5 seconds. Pat into a 7-inch square. Using a 3-inch biscuit cutter dipped in flour, cut out four shortcakes. Quickly gather the scraps and cut out two more. Evenly space them on an ungreased baking sheet. Bake about 12 to 15 minutes, until golden brown. With a spatula, transfer to a rack and let cool about 5 mintues.

5. Meanwhile, prepare the topping: Combine the cream and sugar in a chilled small deep bowl. Using chilled beaters, beat just until soft mounds form. Beat in the vanilla.

6. To serve, split the shortcakes horizontally with a knife. Place a bottom portion in each of six shallow dessert bowls. Stir the berries and spoon about ⅓ cup over each serving. Add the shortcake tops and spoon on another ⅓ cup of the berries. Serve with about 3 tablespoons whipped cream topping each dessert.

KROPSUA (FINNISH DESSERT PANCAKE)

Here is a simple and delicious dessert that
can be put together quickly if you have fresh fruit (or jams or preserves) on hand.
Lingonberries are the traditional topping, but you can use blackberries, peaches,
strawberries, or any fruit you like, sugared ahead of time,
and set aside to draw the juice.

MAKES ONE 9-INCH ROUND PANCAKE (6 SERVINGS)

3 large eggs
3 tablespoons granulated sugar
Pinch of salt
2 cups milk
1 cup all-purpose flour

1 tablespoon confectioner's sugar
Fresh berries or fruit, sweetened if
   desired; or fruit jams or
   preserves

1. Position a rack in the center of the oven and preheat to 425°F. Place a 9-inch cast-iron skillet or a 9-inch cake pan in the oven and heat for 10 minutes.

2. Meanwhile, in a large bowl, whisk the eggs with the sugar and salt. Whisk in the milk and then the flour to make a smooth batter. Remove the hot pan from the oven and quickly brush with vegetable oil to coat lightly. Pour in the batter all at once and bake about 30 minutes, until puffed and golden brown. When removed from the oven, the pancake will collapse immediately. Sift the confectioner's sugar over the top and serve hot with berries, fruit, or preserves.

APPLE PUDDING

A very old-fashioned pudding, somewhere between a betty
and a cobbler, this layered apple dessert is fortified with egg yolks and lightened
with the beaten whites.

MAKES 8 SERVINGS

5 large (6 to 8 ounces each) tart
green apples, such as Granny
Smith, greening, or Baldwin
2 tablespoons fresh lemon juice
4 tablespoons (½ stick) unsalted
butter
3 large eggs, separated
¼ cup milk
1 teaspoon vanilla

⅔ cup granulated sugar
¼ cup all-purpose flour
1 teaspoon baking powder
½ teaspoon ground cinnamon
¼ teaspoon freshly grated nutmeg
Pinch of salt
½ cup (2 ounces) chopped
walnuts
Heavy cream (optional)

1. Position a rack in the center of the oven and preheat to 350°F. Butter a 13-by-9-inch glass baking dish. Peel and core the apples, then cut into ½-inch slices and toss in the baking dish with the lemon juice.

2. In a small pan over low heat, melt the butter.

3. In a medium bowl, whisk together the egg yolks, milk, and vanilla. Whisk in ⅓ cup of the sugar, the flour, baking powder, cinnamon, nutmeg, and salt, and whisk until evenly blended.

4. Remove 1 tablespoon of the remaining ⅓ cup of sugar and toss it with the walnuts on a sheet of waxed paper.

5. In a deep medium-sized bowl beat the egg whites just until soft peaks begin to form. Gradually beat in the remaining sugar and beat until stiff glossy peaks form. Stir a spoonful of the egg whites into the yolk mixture to lighten and then fold the two together. Turn the mixture out over the apples and sprinkle with the walnut-sugar mixture. Bake 30 to 35 minutes, until golden brown on top. Cool for about 15 minutes. Serve warm or at room temperature, with heavy cream if desired.

APPLE BROWN BETTY

This comforting American dessert
makes use of leftover or slightly stale white bread. A beautiful brown color,
it is layered with apple slices and sprinkled with brown sugar. It can be made
ahead and reheated hours later.

MAKES 8 SERVINGS

8 tablespoons (1 stick) unsalted
  butter, sliced
3 cups coarse fresh bread crumbs
  made from firm, homemade-
  style white bread
¾ cup packed dark brown sugar
1 teaspoon ground cinnamon
½ teaspoon freshly grated nutmeg

¼ teaspoon salt
5 large (6 to 8 ounces each) tart
  green apples, such as Granny
  Smith, greening, or Baldwin
1 teaspoon grated lemon zest
2 tablespoons fresh lemon juice
½ cup apple cider or apple juice
Heavy cream (optional)

1. Position a rack in the center of the oven and preheat to 375°F. Generously butter a 13-by-9-inch glass baking dish.

2. In a large heavy skillet melt the butter over moderate heat. Add the bread crumbs and, stirring frequently, heat until toasted a medium golden brown.

3. In a small bowl, stir together the brown sugar, cinnamon, nutmeg, and salt.

4. Peel and core the apples and cut into ¼-inch slices. In a large bowl toss them with the lemon zest, lemon juice, and apple cider.

5. Sprinkle one-fourth of the bread crumbs in the prepared dish. Arrange one-third of the apples and juice over the crumbs and sprinkle with one-third of the sugar mixture and one-third of the remaining crumbs. Repeat twice more. Bake about 45 minutes, until bubbly and browned. Cool about 15 minutes. Serve hot or warm, with heavy cream if desired.

AUNT CHARLOTTE'S APPLE CRISP

One of the best ways to serve tart green apples is in this simple dessert that my Aunt Charlotte made often, all winter long.

MAKES 8 SERVINGS

5 large (6 to 8 ounces each) tart green apples, peeled, cored, and cut into ½-inch slices
1 teaspoon ground cinnamon
1 teaspoon grated nutmeg
½ cup water

¾ cup all-purpose flour
8 tablespoons (1 stick) chilled unsalted butter, sliced
½ cup granulated sugar
½ cup packed light brown sugar
Heavy cream (optional)

1. Position a rack in the center of the oven and preheat to 400°F. In a large bowl, toss the apples with the cinnamon and nutmeg. Turn into an 11¾-by-7½ inch pan, and sprinkle with ½ cup water.

2. In a medium-sized bowl combine the flour, butter, granulated sugar, and brown sugar; with a pastry blender, cut in the butter until the mixture is crumbly and the particles are smaller than peas. Crumble over the apples. Bake 40 to 45 minutes, until golden brown and bubbly. Cool in the pan for about 15 minutes, then serve warm with heavy cream.

BLUEBERRY BUCKLE

This buckle—rather like a cross between a cobbler and a coffee cake—is tasty, colorful, and moist. The berries are mixed right into the batter.

MAKES 9 SQUARES

TOPPING

⅓ cup all-purpose flour
⅓ cup packed light brown sugar
½ teaspoon ground cinnamon

4 tablespoons (½ stick) chilled
  unsalted butter, sliced

BATTER

6 tablespoons (¾ stick) unsalted
  butter, softened
½ cup granulated sugar
1 large egg
1 teaspoon vanilla extract
½ cup sour cream

1¾ cups all-purpose flour
2 teaspoons baking powder
Pinch of salt
1½ cups fresh blueberries, rinsed
  and dried
Heavy cream, for serving

1. Position a rack in the center of the oven and preheat to 375°F. Butter an 8-inch square pan.

2. Prepare the topping: In a small bowl combine the flour, brown sugar, and cinnamon. With a pastry blender, cut in the butter to resemble coarse crumbs.

3. Prepare the batter: In a large bowl, with a handheld electric mixer, beat the butter until creamy. Gradually beat in the sugar until light and fluffy. Add the egg and vanilla and beat until smooth, then beat in the sour cream.

4. In a medium-sized bowl, stir together the flour, baking powder, and salt to evenly blend. Quickly stir the dry ingredients into the butter mixture just to moisten; the batter will be thick and lumpy. Fold in the blueberries and turn into the prepared pan. Crumble the reserved topping over the batter. Bake 30 to 35 minutes, until a toothpick inserted in the cake portion emerges clean. Cool on a rack for 15 to 20 minutes. Cut into 9 squares and serve warm with heavy cream.

PEACH COBBLER

This easily assembled cobbler was frequently popped into the oven
just as our family sat down to dinner. It would be just the right temperature by
the time we were ready to eat it. As with all peach desserts,
it must be made with fully ripe peaches.

MAKES 6 TO 8 SERVINGS

8 medium-sized peaches
  (about 2 pounds)
½ cup granulated sugar
1 tablespoon cornstarch
1 tablespoon unsalted butter

½ teaspoon ground cinnamon
Pinch of salt
½ teaspoon grated lemon zest
1 tablespoon fresh lemon juice

TOPPING

1 cup all-purpose flour
1 tablespoon granulated sugar
1½ teaspoons baking powder
¼ teaspoon salt

3 tablespoons chilled unsalted
  butter, sliced
½ cup milk
Heavy cream for serving (optional)

1. Prepare the peach filling: Bring a medium-sized pot of water to a boil. Add 3 peaches, blanch for 15 to 30 seconds, and then rinse under cold water. Repeat with remaining peaches. Peel, pit and cut into ½-inch slices; you should have 4 cups.

2. Position a rack in the center of the oven and preheat to 400°F. In a large saucepan stir together the sugar and cornstarch, then add the peaches, butter, cinnamon, and salt. Place over moderate heat and bring to a boil, stirring frequently. Remove from the heat and stir in the lemon zest and juice. Turn into an ungreased 8-inch square pan.

3. Prepare the topping: In a medium-sized bowl combine the flour, sugar, baking powder, and salt; then cut in the butter until the mixture resembles coarse meal. Stir in the milk to make a soft dough and drop by the spoonful all over the peach filling. Bake about 20 minutes, until light golden brown. Cool on a rack for at least 15 minutes. Serve warm, with heavy cream if desired.

PEACH AND RASPBERRY CRUNCH

Similar to a cobbler but with a crunchy butter-nut topping,
this special dessert is simple yet elegant. Sometimes we made it
with peaches only, eliminating the raspberries, and we
frequently served it with heavy cream.

MAKES 6 TO 8 SERVINGS

CRUNCHY TOPPING

½ cup (2 ounces) finely chopped
  walnuts or pecans
⅓ cup all-purpose flour
2 tablespoons packed light brown
  sugar

¼ teaspoon ground cinnamon
3 tablespoons unsalted butter,
  softened

FRUIT FILLING

2 large peaches (about 1 pound)
1 pint (2 cups) fresh raspberries
⅓ cup granulated sugar

2 tablespoons all-purpose flour
1 teaspoon vanilla extract

BATTER

¾ cup all-purpose flour
3 tablespoons granulated sugar
1 teaspoon baking powder
Pinch of salt

⅓ cup milk
2 tablespoons unsalted butter,
  melted

1. Adjust a rack to the middle of the oven and preheat to 400°F. Butter an 8-inch square pan.

2. Prepare the crunchy topping: In a small bowl, combine the walnuts, flour, brown sugar, cinnamon, and butter; crumble together with your fingertips until blended.

3. Prepare the fruit filling: Bring a medium-sized pot of water to a boil; add the peaches and blanch for 10 to 15 seconds. Refresh them under cold water, peel, pit, and cut into ½-inch slices. In the prepared pan, toss together the peaches, raspberries, sugar, flour, and vanilla.

4. Prepare the batter: In a medium-sized bowl, stir together the flour, sugar, baking powder, and salt until blended. Add the milk and melted butter and stir quickly just to moisten. Spread the batter over the fruit in a thin layer (it's okay if some of the fruit shows through). Crumble the topping over the batter and bake for about 30 minutes, until bubbly and golden brown. Cool on a rack for about 20 minutes before serving. Serve hot or warm, spooning heavy cream over each serving if desired.

BUTTERED BREAD PUDDING

My mother loved this Old World dessert, which makes use of
stale bread. Best served warm on the day it is made, it is a perfect brunch dish,
reminiscent of french toast.

MAKES 8 TO 12 SERVINGS

10 ½-inch-thick slices challah,
   egg bread, or firm white bread,
   halved (pieces should be about
   3 by 3 inches)
4 tablespoons (½ stick) unsalted
   butter, melted
½ cup raisins
3 large eggs

2 egg yolks
¾ cup granulated sugar
¼ teaspoon ground cinnamon
⅛ teaspoon freshly grated nutmeg
2¼ cups milk
1 cup heavy cream (plus more for
   topping, if desired)
1 teaspoon vanilla extract

1. Lightly toast the bread in a toaster or under the broiler. Brush one side of each slice of toast with melted butter. Butter a 13-by-9-inch glass baking dish, sprinkle in the raisins, and arrange the toast, buttered side up, in tight overlapping rows.

2. In a medium-sized bowl whisk the eggs with the egg yolks. Whisk in the sugar, cinnamon, nutmeg, milk, cream and vanilla. Pour the egg-milk mixture over the buttered toast and let stand for 30 minutes, so the bread soaks up the liquid.

3. Position a rack in the center of the oven and preheat to 350°F. Cover the pudding with aluminum foil and fit the pan into a larger pan (such as a roasting pan) that contains about 1 inch of hot water (see Note page 189). Bake for 30 minutes, then remove foil and bake about 10 minutes longer, until the custard is set. Let rest about 15 minutes before serving. Serve warm, with heavy cream if desired.

RICE PUDDING

Here is a particularly good version of this honest dessert.
Its authentic flavor is accented by cinnamon, nutmeg, and vanilla.
Serve it warm or cold.

MAKES 8 SERVINGS

½ teaspoon salt
½ cup raw long-grain white rice
3 tablespoons unsalted butter
3 large eggs
½ cup granulated sugar
2 teaspoons vanilla extract

¼ teaspoon freshly grated nutmeg
2 cups milk
2 cups half and half
½ cup raisins
½ teaspoon ground cinnamon

1. In a heavy 2-quart saucepan combine 4 cups water and the salt. Place over high heat and bring to a boil. Slowly add the rice so the boiling does not stop and boil for 10 minutes. Drain in a sieve and return to the pan. Add the butter and toss to coat.

2. Position a rack in the center of the oven and preheat to 300°F. Butter an 11¾-by-7½-inch glass baking dish and place it in a larger pan to make a water bath. Pour enough water in the larger pan to come halfway up the sides of the smaller pan. See Note below.

3. In a large bowl, whisk the eggs with the sugar, vanilla, and nutmeg; whisk in the milk and half and half. Stir in the raisins and the rice. Pour into the prepared pan, carefully set the nested pans in the oven, and bake for 45 minutes. Stir the pudding, sprinkle the cinnamon over the top and bake until set, about 45 minutes longer. Cool on a rack and serve warm or chilled.

Note: When using a water bath, or bain-marie, you must be very careful not to scald yourself with the hot water in the outer pan. This is all too easy to do as you remove the paired pans from the oven: The pans are heavy and unless you can keep them absolutely level, the water sloshes around. Use very thick potholders (preferably mitts) and an outer pan with handles, if you have one.

CREAM PUFFS AND ÉCLAIRS

This recipe makes about a dozen and a half cream puffs or éclairs.
Both the cream puff paste (the name generally given to this versatile dough) and
the pastry cream filling may be prepared a day ahead; however, because the
finished pastries do not keep well, it is best to bake and fill them
on the day you wish to serve them.

MAKES ABOUT 1½ DOZEN

CREAM PUFF PASTE

1 cup cold water	½ teaspoon salt
8 tablespoons (1 stick) unsalted butter, sliced	1 cup all-purpose flour
	4 large eggs

PASTRY CREAM

MAKES 3 TO 3½ cups

2 cups milk	4 tablespoons (½ stick) unsalted butter, in pieces
½ cup granulated sugar	
⅓ cup all-purpose flour	2 teaspoons vanilla extract
6 egg yolks	½ cup heavy cream

GLAZE

Pinch of salt	1 egg

TOPPING

2 tablespoons confectioner's sugar (for cream puffs) or	A double recipe (1 cup) Chocolate Glaze (page 203) (for éclairs)

1. Prepare the cream puff paste: In a heavy medium-sized saucepan combine the cold water with the butter and salt. Place over moderate heat and bring to a boil; remove from the heat and stir until the butter has melted. Add the flour all at once and beat with the spoon for about 30 seconds, to dry out slightly. Remove from the heat and beat in the eggs, one at a time, beating well after each addition. The eggs will bind with the flour mixture to make a rather stiff dough that "cleans the

bowl." If not using the paste right away, cover it with plastic wrap placed directly on the surface. The paste can be held at room temperature for several hours or refrigerated a day or two.

2. Lightly grease and flour two baking sheets. Evenly space two racks in the oven and preheat to 450°F

3. To make éclairs: Fit a large pastry bag with a ½- to ¾-inch plain tip; fill with the cream puff paste. Squeeze out strips of dough that are ¾ to 1 inch wide and 4 to 5 inches long, leaving 1½ inches between them.

4. For the glaze, add a pinch of salt to the egg, stir with a fork, then brush glaze over the tops of the strips. Draw the tines of a fork lengthwise over each one to leave ridges about ⅛ inch deep, which will help them puff more during baking. Bake until puffed and golden, 8 to 10 minutes. Reduce the heat to 400°F and bake 5 minutes longer. Reduce the heat to 300°F and bake until dry, 15 to 20 minutes more. Remove from the oven and poke a small hole in both ends of each éclair, using a chopstick or a knife tip. Cool on a rack.

5. To make cream puffs: Fit a large pastry bag with a ½-inch plain tip and fill with the cream puff paste. Squeeze out balls of the paste onto the prepared baking sheets, making them about 1½ inches in diameter and spacing them about 1½ inches apart. Brush the tops with the egg glaze (see Step 4). Bake until puffed and golden, about 10 minutes. Reduce the heat to 400°F and bake 5 minutes longer. Reduce the heat to 300°F and bake until dry, 15 to 20 minutes more. Remove from the oven and poke a small hole in each cream puff, using a chopstick or a knife tip. Cool on a rack. The empty éclairs or puffs can be stored in a covered container for a day or two before they are filled.

6. Prepare the pastry cream: In a medium-sized heavy saucepan over low heat, scald the milk just until tiny bubbles form around the edges of the surface.

7. In a heavy medium-sized saucepan stir together the sugar and flour. Whisk in the hot milk in a steady stream, blending until smooth. Cook over moderate heat, stirring constantly, until thickened and boiling. Reduce the heat and simmer over low heat for 2 to 3 minutes.

8. Whisk the egg yolks in a medium-sized bowl and whisk in about 2 cups of the hot mixture. Return to the saucepan containing the rest of the hot mixture and simmer 2 or 3 minutes longer, until thickened further. Remove from the heat and stir in the butter and vanilla, continuing to stir until the butter melts. Turn into a bowl, cover with plastic wrap placed directly on the surface, and cool to room temperature.

9. Using a chilled small deep bowl and chilled beaters, whip the cream until stiff. Fold into the cooled pastry cream to lighten it. Chill.

10. If you have made éclairs, prepare a double recipe (1 cup) of chocolate glaze.

11. To fill éclairs and cream puffs: With a sharp knife, slice off the top third of the puffs or éclairs. With a spoon, fill them with pastry cream, mounding it slightly. Replace the tops. Sift the confectioner's sugar over the cream puffs; spread chocolate glaze over the éclairs. Serve, chilled, within two hours after filling them.

CREAM HORNS

These cream horns make a beautiful dessert—cones of flaky puff pastry filled with blackberry jam and whipped cream, dusted with confectioner's sugar. Note that you will need at least six, preferably twelve, 4- to 4½-inch metal horn molds or cornucopia molds.

MAKES 1 DOZEN

HORNS

1 pound puff pastry, partially
    thawed if frozen (see Note)
1 large egg

1 teaspoon water
2 teaspoons granulated sugar

CREAM FILLING

1¼ cups heavy cream
¼ cup sifted confectioner's sugar
1 teaspoon vanilla extract

¼ cup blackberry, boysenberry, or
    raspberry jam

TOPPING

1 teaspoon confectioner's sugar

1. Line two baking sheets with baker's parchment and lightly grease the parchment.

2. Prepare the horns: On a lightly floured surface, roll out ½ pound of the puff pastry to a rectangle that measures 9 by 12 inches. Cutting crosswise with a long sharp knife and using a pressing (rather than sawing) motion, cut the pastry into 12 strips, each 1 inch wide and 9 inches long. Keep them on a lightly floured board in the refrigerator until needed. You will need two strips for each horn. Lightly brush two strips, on one side only, with cold water. Beginning at the point of a 4- to 4½-inch metal horn mold, wrap one strip, moistened side out, around the mold; once the tip is secure and the dough overlaps, the wrapping will be easy. If you have trouble getting started, try this method: Place one of the moistened strips, wet side down, on your work surface; hold the point of the mold at one end and roll it, holding the dough to the mold at the point. Once it has overlapped, press the dough so it holds and then carefully pick up the mold and the dough strip and wrap it around and around, each time overlapping by ¼ inch. When one strip has been wrapped, pick up the second one and overlap the end of the first one by about ¼ inch; press lightly together and continue wrapping in the same manner. When done, place with best side up on a prepared baking sheet. Repeat to make 6; refrigerate for 30 minutes.

3. While the first set of horns is chilling, roll out the second half-pound of pastry and make another 6 horns, placing them on the second baking sheet and refrigerating the finished horns for 30 minutes.

4. Position a rack in the lower third of the oven and preheat to 425°F. Using a fork, beat the egg with 1 teaspoon water to make a glaze. Brush each horn with some glaze and lightly sprinkle with sugar, using 1 teaspoon for 6. Place one sheet of chilled and glazed horns in the oven and bake for 10 minutes, until puffed. Reduce the temperature to 350°F and bake an additional 8 to 10 minutes, until golden brown. Remove from the oven and return the temperature to 425°F to bake the second sheet. While the baked horns are still hot, twist the molds gently to make sure that they do not stick, but leave them inside until cool. Bake the second batch as before, lowering the oven temperature to 350°F after 10 minutes.

5. When all of the horns have cooled, remove the molds. Bake the unmolded horns at 300°F for 10 to 15 minutes to dry the pastry. Cool completely on a rack before filling.

6. Prepare the filling: Using chilled beaters and bowl, beat the cream with an electric mixer until soft peaks start to form; add the sugar and beat just until stiff. Stir in the vanilla.

7. With a small spatula or butter knife, spread 1 teaspoon of the jam inside each horn.

8. You can fill the horns by using a pastry bag and a ½-inch star tip or with a knife or small spatula. Fill the horns, making a star design at the end or scraping the cream off flat with a knife. Sift the confectioner's sugar over them all at once for a *very* light topping. Serve chilled.

Note: Many fine bakers will sell puff pastry by the pound. It is difficult and time-consuming to make. You may also substitute frozen puff pastry. When purchasing, look for a brand that contains butter, as puff pastry should. Some brands contain none, which makes them less than ideal.

NEW YORK CHEESECAKE

This recipe makes a thick and rich cheesecake that has no crust to get soggy. I recommend that you chill it overnight before slicing it.

MAKES ONE 10-INCH CHEESECAKE

5 large eggs
2 cups (1 pint) sour cream
Four 8-ounce packages cream
 cheese
8 tablespoons (1 stick) unsalted
 butter

1½ cups granulated sugar
2 tablespoons cornstarch
1½ teaspoons vanilla extract
1 teaspoon fresh lemon juice
1 teaspoon grated lemon zest

1. Let the eggs, sour cream, cream cheese, and butter come to room temperature. Adjust a rack to the center of the oven and preheat to 300°F. Generously butter a 10-inch springform pan. To ensure that no moisture from the water bath seeps into the pan, wrap a double layer of heavy-duty aluminum foil tightly around the bottom and sides, crimping and pleating the foil to make it conform. Fold the top edge of the foil down so it is even with the top edge of the pan.

2. In a large mixing bowl, using an electric mixer, beat the eggs with the sour cream until well blended.

3. In a medium-sized bowl, beat the cream cheese with the butter until smooth and creamy. Scrape into the egg-sour cream mixture and beat until smooth. Add the sugar, cornstarch, vanilla, lemon juice, and lemon zest and beat thoroughly, about 2 minutes. Pour into the prepared springform pan and place in a roasting pan large enough to prevent the sides from touching. Place in the oven and carefully pour in enough very hot tap water to reach halfway up the sides of the springform pan.

4. Bake for 2 hours 15 minutes, or until the cake is very lightly colored and a knife inserted in the center emerges clean. Remove from the water bath (see Note, page 189) and carefully peel the aluminum foil from around the pan. Let stand at room temperature until completely cool, about 4 hours. Refrigerate, covered, until well chilled.

FROSTINGS AND GLAZES

OLD-FASHIONED BUTTERCREAM

Because this frosting begins with a base
thickened with potato starch (see page 14), it is not as sweet as many other
buttercreams. This makes it a perfect counterpoint to a rich cake
like the pecan layer cake.

MAKES 3½ CUPS

3 tablespoons potato starch
1 cup cold milk
2 egg yolks
1½ cups sifted confectioner's
   sugar

1¼ cups (2½ sticks) unsalted
   butter, softened
1 tablespoon vanilla extract

1. Place the potato starch in a small heavy saucepan. Gradually whisk in the milk until smooth, and then whisk in the egg yolks and 1 cup of the confectioner's sugar. Place over moderately low heat and, stirring constantly, cook until the mixture becomes very thick and begins to boil, about 10 minutes. Turn this buttercream base into a shallow dish, cover with plastic wrap placed directly on the surface, and cool to room temperature.

2. In a large bowl combine the butter and remaining ½ cup confectioner's sugar; beat until light and fluffy, 1 to 2 minutes. Using an electric mixer with a very strong motor, preferably an upright model, beat in the buttercream base bit by bit, beating until smooth. Beat in the vanilla. Use to frost cakes at room temperature; the frosting will set when chilled.

ORANGE BUTTERCREAM:

1. Beat in 2 teaspoons grated orange zest and 2 tablespoons orange liqueur.

CHOCOLATE BUTTER FROSTING

Use this chocolate-rich and buttery frosting to fill and frost Aunt Charlotte's milk chocolate cake, and carnival cake, among others.

MAKES 3½ TO 4 CUPS

5 ounces (5 squares) unsweetened chocolate, chopped
1 cup (2 sticks) unsalted butter, softened

3½ cups sifted confectioner's sugar
2 large eggs, lightly beaten
1½ teaspoons vanilla extract

1. Melt the chocolate in the top of a double boiler over barely simmering water. Cool to room temperature.

2. Place the butter in a large bowl and beat with an electric mixer until fluffy, about 1 minute. Gradually beat in the sugar alternately with the eggs and vanilla. Beat in the cooled chocolate to make a frosting of good spreading consistency. Use at room temperature; the frosting will set if chilled.

FLUFFY BURNT BUTTER FROSTING

This buttercreamlike frosting derives its flavor
and color from butter that is browned, chilled, softened to room temperature,
then beaten until fluffy with confectioner's sugar and milk.
It's wonderful on burnt butter cupcakes.

MAKES ABOUT 2 CUPS

8 tablespoons (1 stick) unsalted butter
2 tablespoons vegetable shortening

3 cups sifted confectioner's sugar
2 to 3 tablespoons milk
1 teaspoon vanilla extract

1. Place the butter in a small heavy skillet over moderate heat; melt, stirring frequently, and cook until deep golden brown, about 3 minutes. Pour into a small bowl, cool to room temperature, cover, and chill until solid. Soften to room temperature before proceeding.

2. In a deep medium-sized bowl combine the softened burnt butter and the shortening; beat with an electric mixer until fluffy, about 1 minute. Continue to beat and gradually beat in enough sugar so the mixture is stiff. Then add the remaining sugar alternately with 2 tablespoons of milk, drop by drop, and the vanilla. If necessary beat in drops of the remaining milk to make a fluffy frosting of good spreading consistency. Use at room temperature or frosting will set.

GRANDMA'S FUDGE FROSTING

This thick, fudgy, not too sweet frosting begins
with a granulated sugar and heavy cream mixture that is simmered for ten minutes
before the chocolate is added, and then cooled to an ideal spreading consistency.
Sublime on grandma's devil's food cake and equally good
over almost any cake of your choice.

MAKES 3 CUPS

1½ cups granulated sugar
1 cup heavy cream
6 ounces (6 squares)
   unsweetened chocolate,
   coarsely chopped

8 tablespoons (1 stick) unsalted
   butter, sliced
2 teaspoons vanilla extract

1. In a heavy medium-sized saucepan combine the sugar and heavy cream. Place over moderate heat and, stirring constantly, bring to a boil. Reduce the heat and simmer for 10 minutes without stirring. Remove from the heat and stir in the chocolate, butter, and vanilla, continuing to stir until chocolate and butter melt. Turn into a bowl and cool to room temperature, stirring occasionally. Refrigerate, stirring frequently, until thickened and of a good spreading consistency. Use to frost a cake before the frosting sets completely.

BUTTERSCOTCH BUTTERCREAM

This frosting with a deep butterscotch flavor is particularly good
with the country apple cake.

MAKES 3 CUPS

3 large eggs
1 cup packed dark brown sugar
1½ cups (3 sticks) unsalted
   butter, at room temperature

2 teaspoons vanilla extract

1. Choose a large bowl, preferably a stainless steel one, that will partially fit into a large saucepan. Fill the pan with 1 inch of water and bring to a boil over moderate heat. Reduce the heat and keep at a simmer.

2. In the large bowl whisk the eggs until frothy. Add the brown sugar and whisk until smooth. Place over the simmering water (the bowl should not touch the water) and whisk constantly until the mixture is just slightly warm and the grains of sugar have dissolved, 1 to 2 minutes. Remove the bowl from the pan and cool to room temperature, stirring occasionally.

3. Place the butter in a deep medium-sized bowl and beat with an electric mixer until fluffy. Gradually beat in the cooled sugar mixture until smooth and fluffy, then beat in the vanilla. Use right away to frost a cake. The buttercream will set when chilled.

LEMON BUTTERCREAM

Tart and tangy with a pronounced lemon flavor, this old-fashioned meringue
buttercream is perfect for frosting a tart lemon layer cake.

MAKES ABOUT 3 CUPS

3 large egg whites (½ cup)
1 cup granulated sugar
1 cup (2 sticks) unsalted butter,
   at cool room temperature

1 tablespoon grated lemon zest
⅓ cup fresh lemon juice

1. Choose a large bowl, preferably a stainless steel one, that will partially fit into a large saucepan. Fill the pan with 1 inch of water and bring the water to a simmer over moderate heat. Reduce the heat and keep at a simmer. Combine the egg whites and sugar in the bowl and whisk just until the mixture is warm and the sugar has dissolved; remove from the heat.

2. Using an electric mixer (preferably an upright model with a strong motor), beat the egg white mixture until stiff glossy peaks form. The mixture should not be warm; if it is, beat until it is cool. Cut the butter into tablespoon-size slices. One at a time, beat them in, beating well after each addition. After all of the butter has been added, beat just until smooth. If the buttercream "breaks" (begins to separate), continue beating at high speed until smooth. If the frosting is still broken, chill for 10 to 15 minutes and beat again.

3. Add the lemon zest and, while beating at medium speed, gradually beat in the lemon juice. Beat at high speed, just until smooth. Use right away to frost the lemon layer cake.

CREAM CHEESE FROSTING

This popular and delicious frosting is not too sweet.
Traditionally used on carrot cake, it also marries perfectly with banana-pineapple cake and maraschino cherry cake.

MAKES 2⅔ CUPS

One 8-ounce package cream
  cheese, softened
4 tablespoons (½ stick) unsalted
  butter, softened

3 cups sifted confectioner's sugar
1 teaspoon vanilla extract

1. In a large bowl combine the cream cheese and butter; beat with an electric mixer until fluffy, about 1 minute. Beat in the sugar, one cup at a time, until smooth. Beat in the vanilla.

2. Place the bowl of frosting in the refrigerator and chill, stirring frequently, just until thick enough to be of a good spreading consistency. Frost the cake and chill to set.

Seven-Minute Caramel Frosting

"Seven-minute" frostings are fluffy frostings
based on egg whites and sugar that have been whipped into billows of meringuelike
consistency and heated over simmering water. In this version,
brown sugar imparts a caramel flavor.

MAKES 5 TO 6 CUPS

¾ cup packed dark brown sugar
½ teaspoon cream of tartar
Pinch of salt
2 large egg whites

¼ cup cold water
2 teaspoons vanilla extract
1 cup (4 ounces) chopped
walnuts

1. Choose a large stainless steel or heatproof glass bowl that will fit over, not in, a medium-sized saucepan. Bring about 1 inch of water to a simmer in the pan.

2. In the bowl, combine the sugar, cream of tartar, salt, egg whites, and cold water. Place over the simmering water and beat with a handheld electric mixer until the frosting is fluffy and stands in stiff peaks, about 6 minutes. Remove the bowl from the water and beat, off the heat, for 1 minute longer. Beat in the vanilla and fold in the walnuts. Use immediately to frost a cake.

Fluffy Maple Frosting

Pure maple syrup is combined with sugar and egg whites and whipped over
simmering water to make this delicious fluffy frosting.

MAKES 4½ TO 5 CUPS

½ cup pure Vermont maple syrup
½ cup granulated sugar
2 large egg whites

¼ teaspoon salt
2 teaspoons vanilla extract

1. Choose a large stainless steel or heatproof glass bowl that will fit over, not in, a medium-sized saucepan. Fill the pan with about 1 inch of water and bring to a simmer.

2. In the bowl, off the heat, combine the maple syrup, sugar, egg whites, and salt. Place over the simmering water and beat with a handheld electric mixer until the frosting is fluffy and stands in stiff peaks, about 6 minutes. Remove the bowl from the water and beat for about 1 minute longer. Beat in the vanilla. Use immediately to frost cooled cake layers.

PECAN-COCONUT FROSTING

This lovely crunchy frosting is the classic topping for German chocolate cake, but it is equally good with dark chocolate cakes and with yellow cakes.

MAKES 3½ CUPS

1 cup granulated sugar
1 cup heavy cream
3 large eggs, lightly beaten
8 tablespoons (1 stick) unsalted butter, sliced

1½ cups (6 ounces) chopped pecans
1 cup (about 3 ounces) sweetened shredded coconut
1 teaspoon vanilla extract

1. In a heavy medium-sized saucepan combine the sugar, cream, eggs, and butter. Place over moderate heat and, stirring constantly, cook until the mixture thickens and just begins to boil, about 10 minutes. Remove from the heat and stir in the pecans, coconut, and vanilla. Transfer to a bowl and cool to room temperature, stirring occasionally, until thick enough to fill and frost a cake.

BURNT BUTTER GLAZE

Sweet butter browned in a skillet intensifies in flavor, while developing characteristic dark specks. The addition of sugar and milk complete this delicious glaze.

MAKES 1 CUP

4 tablespoons (½ stick) unsalted
butter, softened
2 cups sifted confectioner's sugar

2 to 3 tablespoons milk
1 teaspoon vanilla extract

1. Place the butter in a small heavy skillet over moderate heat. Melt, stirring frequently, and cook until deep golden brown, about 3 minutes. Pour into a medium-sized bowl. Stir in 1 cup of the confectioner's sugar until dissolved. Gradually stir in 2 tablespoons of the milk and the vanilla until smooth. Stir in the remaining cup of sugar and enough of the remaining milk, drop by drop, to make a glaze. Cover, or use right away.

CHOCOLATE GLAZE

Drizzle this simple and tasty glaze over the afternoon tea cakes or over any cake that's been frosted with seven-minute caramel frosting.

MAKES ½ CUP

1 tablespoon unsalted butter
2 tablespoons water
½ ounce (½ square) unsweetened
chocolate

1 cup sifted confectioner's sugar
¼ teaspoon ground cinnamon
1 teaspoon vanilla extract

1. In a small saucepan combine the butter with 2 tablespoons water. Place over low heat, add the chocolate, and stir until the chocolate melts and the mixture thickens slightly; remove from the heat.

2. In a small bowl combine the confectioner's sugar and cinnamon; stir in the chocolate mixture and the vanilla to make a smooth glaze.

List of Illustrations

INDEX